IN THE NAME OF

ALLAH

THE ALL-COMPASSIONATE, ALL-MERCIFUL

THE WORLD OF THE NOBLE ANGELS

- Title: THE WORLD OF THE NOBLE ANGELS
- Author: 'Umar S. al-Ashqar
- Arabic Edition 1 (1990)
- Translated from Arabic edition 7 (1995)
- English Edition 2 (2005)
- Translator: Nasiruddin al-Khattab
- Editor: Huda Khattab
- Layout: IIPH, Riyadh, Saudi Arabia
- Cover Designer: Haroon Vicente Pascual, Arlington, U.S.A.

ISLAMIC CREED SERIES 2

THE WORLD OF THE NOBLE ANGELS

In the Light of the Qur'an and Sunnah

'Umar S. al-Ashqar

Translated by:
Nasiruddin al-Khattab

INTERNATIONAL ISLAMIC PUBLISHING HOUSE

King Fahd National Library Cataloging-in-Publication Data

Al-Ashqar, Umar S.

The world of the Noble Angels in the light of the Qur'an and Sunnah. / Umar S. al-Ashqar ; translated by Nasiruddin al-Khattab - 2nd ed.,-Riyadh , 2005

...p ; 22 cm ,- **(Islamic creed series ; 2)**

1- Angels (Islamic creed) I-Nasiruddin al-Khattab (trans.)
II-Title III-Series

243 dc 5383/22

Legal Deposit no. **5383/22**
ISBN Hard Cover: **9960-672-75-1**
ISBN Soft Cover: **9960-672-93-X**

International Islamic Publishing House (IIPH)

P.O.Box 55195 Riyadh 11534, Saudi Arabia
Tel: 966 1 4650818 - 4647213 - Fax: 4633489
E-Mail: iiph@iiph.com.sa . www.iiph.com.sa

---

*Please take part in this noble work by conveying your comments to **IIPH** through e-mail, fax or postal-mail address.*

TABLE OF CONTENTS

PUBLISHER'S NOTE

All praise and thanks belong to Allah, Lord of the Universe. May Allah's blessings and peace be upon the last of the prophets and messengers Muhammad, his family, Companions, and all those who follow his footsteps till the end of time.

This is the second book of the Islamic Creed (*'aqeedah*) series by Dr. 'Umar Sulaymaan al-Ashqar. It deals with the world of the Angels, an integral part of the Islamic faith. Persons denying the existence of Angels go outside the pale of Islam.

As usual, Dr. Al-Ashqar has discussed this issue exhaustively. His arguments are based on the texts of the Qur'an and the Sunnah. He has covered all aspects of the topic: definition, origin and characteristics, kinds and their relationship with mankind and other creation. Moreover, he draws a comparison between mankind and the angels in their respective roles as determined by Allah. A number of editions of the Arabic original have been sold out.

We are pleased to present this excellent English translation of a very popular book. May Allah bless with acceptance the efforts of the author, the translator and all those associated with the publication of this work.

Muhammad ibn 'Abdul-Muḥsin Al Tuwaijri
General Manager
International Islamic Publishing House
Riyadh, Saudi Arabia

TRANSLATOR'S FOREWORD

In the name of Allah, the Most Gracious, the Most Merciful

Belief in the Unseen *(Al-Ghayb)* is one of the basic tenets of Islam, and forms an important part of Islamic teachings. One of the unseen worlds of which Islam tells us is the world of the angels, who are described in great detail in the Qur'an and Sunnah and who are involved with man throughout his life.

From the moment an individual is conceived in his mother's womb, until his death and beyond, angels play a role in human life. Angels accompany the human being, protecting him and keeping a record of all his deeds. Angels bring forth the soul of the deceased person/s and they bring comfort or inflict torment in the grave. An angel will sound the Trumpet on the Last Day, and angels will be present on the Day of Judgement until they accompany people to their ultimate destination in Paradise or Hell.

Almost all human cultures, ancient and modern, have some kind of belief about angels. The pre-Islamic Arabs believed them to be daughters of the Almighty. Some philosophers thought that angels were the stars in the sky. In modern times there has been a resurgence of interest in angels, and they feature prominently in movies and other forms of popular western culture. Stories featuring angels circulate on the internet and various kinds of gifts, bearing supposed images of angels, gift shops in the west.

But these myths have no role to play in the belief of the Muslim. Our beliefs are based on the teachings of the Qur'an and Sunnah, which tell us all we need to know about the reality of the unseen, including the world of the angels. Belief in the angels brings comfort to man's soul; this belief makes man feel that he is important in the sight of Allah, and that he matters a lot to Him; this belief also encourages a person to strive in the path of goodness. Hence it is of the utmost importance for the

Muslim to understand what Islam says about the angels, and what the implications of this knowledge are for his daily life. In this book, Dr. 'Umar al-Ashqar draws on the sources of Islam to give us a comprehensive picture of who the angels are, their origins, their role in the universe and their interaction with mankind in this world and the next.

May Allah reward the author for his presentation of the Islamic belief in the angels. May He guide us on the Straight Path which leads to Paradise, and may He grant us admittance to that eternal abode where the angels will welcome the believers with greetings of *salaam*. May Allah bless our Prophet Muhammad and his family and Companions, and grant them peace.

Naṣiruddin al-Khaṭṭab

Translator's Note:

All translations of the meaning of the Qur'anic quotations have been taken from "Translation of the Meanings of the Noble Qur'an" by Dr. Muhammad Muḥsin Khan and Dr. Muhammad Taqi-ud-Din al-Hilali, unless otherwise stated.

AUTHOR'S FOREWORD

Praise be to Allah. We praise Him and seek His help, forgiveness and guidance. We seek refuge in Allah from the evil of our own selves and from our evil actions. Whomsoever Allah guides, none can lead astray, and whomsoever He leads astray, none can guide. I bear witness that there is no god except Allah alone, with no associate or partner, and I bear witness that Muhammad is His slave and Messenger.

Belief in the angels is one of the basic principles of *'aqeedah*, and faith is not complete without this belief. The angels form one of the worlds of the Unseen, belief in which is commanded by Allah, Who praises those who believe in what Allah and His Messenger (ﷺ) have told us about them.

The texts of the Qur'an and Sunnah speak in detail about all aspects of this subject. Whoever studies these texts will come to have a clear belief in the angels and realize that this is not an obscure topic. This will deepen and strengthen his faith, for detailed knowledge is stronger and firmer than general knowledge.

The only reason why the texts go into such detail on this topic is that the human mind on its own is not able to learn about the angels. Human senses are unable to see the angels or hear their conversations, but this inability is no doubt in man's best interests, for if man could hear and see everything that is going on around him, he would not be able to survive. It is sufficient for us to imagine how hard it would be for a man if he could detect all the sounds that are picked up by a radio set; the result would surely make him lose his mind.

No one should assume that studying this principle is a kind of superfluous knowledge. The facts stated in the texts which speak of this topic have a great effect in counteracting the myths and false beliefs that exist in people's minds concerning this matter. Since ancient times there has been a widespread belief that the angels are divine or that they are the daughters of Allah, and some philosophers think that the angels are the stars which we see in space.

The facts which are stated in the texts implant in our hearts the firm belief in the One God Who is in control of all of creation, Who has appointed His troops of angels to take care of the various affairs of this universe.

The relationship of the angels with us, their role in our formation and their watching over us, speaks to man of his importance and valuable status, and it refutes the idea that human beings are insignificant and worthless. Thus man can fully appreciate his own value and strive hard to play the great role which he is required to fulfil.

If we were to count the positive effects which stem from man's belief in the angels, and to study the texts which speak of them, the introduction would turn into a lenghty article. So I will leave the reader to look at those texts which, when studied in depth, will supply him with these inspiring effects.

We ask Allah to benefit people through this book, and to make it sincerely for His sake, for He is the best of helpers and supporters.

'Umar Sulaymaan al-Ashqar

INTRODUCTION
DEFINITION OF THE ANGELS AND BELIEF IN THEM

The Angels form a world different to the world of mankind and the world of the jinn. It is a noble world, completely pure. They are noble and pious, worshipping Allah as He should be worshipped, fulfilling whatever He commands them to do and never disobeying Him.

From the texts of the Qur'an and Sunnah, we will see their attributes as described therein.

The word *malak* (angel) is derived from the root *alaka*; *ma'lakah* and *ma'lak* mean message. From this root is derived the word *malaa'ik* (angels), because they are the messengers of Allah.

It is also said that the word *malak* is derived from the root *la'aka*, and that *mal'aakah* means message. The phrase *wa'alikni ila fulaan* means 'convey to him from me.' *Al-Mal'ak* means *al-malak* (angel) because the angels convey (messages) from Allah.

Some of the scholars said *al-malak* (angel) is derived from *al-mulk* (sovereignty). He said: if one of the angels is in control of some affairs, he is described as *malak*, and if a human being is in control of some affairs, he is described as *malik* (king).[1]

Belief in the angels is one of the principles of faith. A person's faith cannot be correct unless he believes in them. Allah says:

﴿ءَامَنَ ٱلرَّسُولُ بِمَآ أُنزِلَ إِلَيْهِ مِن رَّبِّهِۦ وَٱلْمُؤْمِنُونَ ۚ كُلٌّ ءَامَنَ بِٱللَّهِ وَمَلَـٰٓئِكَتِهِۦ وَكُتُبِهِۦ وَرُسُلِهِۦ لَا نُفَرِّقُ بَيْنَ أَحَدٍ مِّن رُّسُلِهِۦ ۚ ﴿٢٨٥﴾﴾

﴿The Messenger [Muhammad] believes in what has been sent down to him from his Lord, and [so do] the believers. Each one believes in

---

[1] *Baṣaa'ir Dhawi al-Tamyeez*, by Al-Fayroozabadi, 4/524.

Allah, His Angels, His Books, and His Messengers. [They say,] 'We make no distinction between one another of His Messengers.'》
(Qur'an 2:285)

How should we believe in the angels?

Suyooṭi narrated that Al-Bayhaqi said in *Shu'ab al-Eemaan*: "Belief in the Angels" means the following:

1. Belief that they exist.
2. Giving each one of them his rightful status, and believing that they are the slaves of Allah, created by Him, like mankind and the jinn. They are commanded to do things and they are accountable. They are not able to do anything except that which Allah has enabled them to do. Death is possible for them, but Allah gives them a long life, and they do not die until their appointed time comes. They should not be described in any way that would imply association with Allah, and they should not be regarded as gods as they were regarded by the ancients, some traditional cultures of early people.
3. Acknowledging that among them are messengers whom Allah sends to whomsoever He wills among mankind. He may also send some of them to others. This implies acknowledging that among them are the bearers of the Throne, those who stand in ranks, the keepers of Paradise, the keepers of Hell, those who record man's deeds and those who drive the clouds. The Qur'an has mentioned all or most of them."[2]

This book will describe in detail what is said in the texts (of the Qur'an and Sunnah) about belief in the angels.

---

[2] *Al-Ḥabaa'ik fi Akhbaar al-Malaa'ik* by Suyooṭi, Pp. 10. See *Mukhtaṣar Shu'ab al-Eemaan*, 1/405-406.

CHAPTER ONE
THEIR PHYSICAL CHARACTERISTICS, ATTRIBUTES AND ABILITIES

In this chapter we look at what we have learned from the *ṣaḥeeḥ* texts about the physical characteristics as well as the attributes of the angels, then we will discuss the abilities which Allah has granted to them.

1 - PHYSICAL CHARACTERISTICS

(1) What they were created from and when

The substance from which Allah created them is light. In *Ṣaḥeeḥ Muslim* it is narrated from 'Aa'ishah (may Allah be pleased with her and her father) that the Messenger of Allah (ﷺ) said: "The angels were created from light, the jinn were created from smokeless fire, and Adam was created from that which has been described to you."[1]

The Messenger (ﷺ) did not explain what light this is that they were created from. Hence we cannot indulge in trying to say more about this matter, because it is the matter of the unseen concerning which no further clarification has been narrated, apart from this hadith.

It is narrated that 'Ikrimah said: "The angels were created from the light of glory and *Iblees* was created from the fire of glory." And it is narrated that 'Abd-Allah ibn 'Amr said, "Allah created the angels from the light of the arms and chest." It is not permissible to accept these views, even if they are narrated through sound chains from these scholars, because they are not infallible, and they may have taken these ideas from the

---

[1] Muslim, 4/2294, hadith no. 2996.

Some of those who claim to be scholars reject this hadith and others like it, claiming that it is a hadith *aaḥaad*, and that a hadith *aaḥaad* cannot be relied on in matters of *'aqeedah*. I have criticized this view and explained its flawed nature in a paper entitled *Aṣl al-I'tiqaad*.

Israa'eeliyyaat (reports from Jewish sources).[2]

Wali-Ullah ad-Dehlawi said: "The hosts on high (the angels) are of three groups: a group upon whom Allah made the system of goodness was dependent, so He created them from physical light similar to the fire of Moosa and breathed into them noble souls;

A group which was created from a mixture of very light vapour and other elements, which resulted in the emergence of great souls with a strong aversion to animalistic behaviour;

And a group of human souls who are very close to the hosts on high, who keep striving to do deeds which could save them and help them to catch up with (the angels), until they shed their physical cloaks and follow in their footsteps, and are counted as being among them."

There is no *ṣaḥeeḥ* evidence to support this definition and this division of the angels into these categories.

We do not know when the angels were created, for Allah has not informed us about that. But we do know that they were created before Adam, the father of mankind. Allah has told us that He informed the angels that He was going to create a *khaleefah* on earth:

﴿وَإِذْ قَالَ رَبُّكَ لِلْمَلَٰٓئِكَةِ إِنِّي جَاعِلٌ فِي ٱلْأَرْضِ خَلِيفَةً ۖ ﴿٣٠﴾﴾

﴾Behold, your Lord said to the angels, 'I will create a vicegerent *[khaleefah]* on earth.'﴿ *(Qur'an 2:30* - A. Yoosuf 'Ali)

What is meant by the word *khaleefah* here is Adam (عليه السلام), and He commanded them to prostrate to him when He created him:

﴿فَإِذَا سَوَّيْتُهُۥ وَنَفَخْتُ فِيهِ مِن رُّوحِى فَقَعُوا۟ لَهُۥ سَٰجِدِينَ ﴿٢٩﴾﴾

﴾'So, when I have fashioned him completely and breathed into him [Adam] the soul which I created for him, then fall [you] down prostrating yourselves unto him.'﴿ *(Qur'an 15:29)*

---

[2] *Silsilat al-Aḥaadeeth aṣ-Ṣaḥeeḥah,* 1/197.

Seeing the angels

Because the angels have bodies of light which are of a low density, mankind cannot see them, especially since Allah has not given our eyes the ability to see them.

No one among this ummah has seen the angels in their true form apart from the Messenger (ﷺ). He saw Jibreel twice in the form in which Allah created him. The texts indicate that human beings are able to see the angels when the angels appear in human form.

(2) Their great physical size

Allah says concerning the angels of Hell:

﴿يَٰٓأَيُّهَا ٱلَّذِينَ ءَامَنُوا۟ قُوٓا۟ أَنفُسَكُمْ وَأَهْلِيكُمْ نَارًا وَقُودُهَا ٱلنَّاسُ وَٱلْحِجَارَةُ عَلَيْهَا مَلَٰٓئِكَةٌ غِلَاظٌ شِدَادٌ لَّا يَعْصُونَ ٱللَّهَ مَآ أَمَرَهُمْ وَيَفْعَلُونَ مَا يُؤْمَرُونَ ۝٦﴾

﴾O you who believe! Ward off yourselves and your families against a Fire [Hell] whose fuel is men and stones, over which are [appointed] angels stern [and] severe, who disobey not, [from executing] the Commands they receive from Allah, but do that which they are commanded.﴿ *(Qur'an 66:6)*

It will be sufficient to quote the *aḥaadeeth* which speak of two noble angels.

The great size of Jibreel (عليه السلام)

The Messenger of Allah (ﷺ) saw Jibreel twice in the angelic form in which Allah created him. These two occasions are mentioned in the *aayaat*:

﴿وَلَقَدْ رَءَاهُ بِٱلْأُفُقِ ٱلْمُبِينِ ۝٢٣﴾

﴾And indeed he [Muhammad] saw him [Jibreel] in the clear horizon [towards the east].﴿ *(Qur'an 81:23)*

And:

﴿وَلَقَدْ رَءَاهُ نَزْلَةً أُخْرَىٰ ﴿١٣﴾ عِندَ سِدْرَةِ ٱلْمُنتَهَىٰ ﴿١٤﴾ عِندَهَا جَنَّةُ ٱلْمَأْوَىٰٓ ﴿١٥﴾﴾

﴾And indeed he [Muhammad] saw him [Jibreel] at a second descent [i.e. another time].
Near *Sidrat-ul-Muntaha* [a lote tree of the utmost boundary over the seventh heaven beyond which none can pass].
Near it is the Paradise of Abode.﴿ *(Qur'an 53:13-15)*

- that was when he was taken up to the highest heaven (during the *Mi'raaj*).

In *Ṣaḥeeḥ Muslim* it is narrated that 'Aa'ishah (may Allah be pleased with her) said: "I asked the Messenger of Allah (ﷺ) about these two *aayaat.* He said, 'That is Jibreel; I never saw him in the form in which Allah created him except on these two occasions. I saw him descending from the heavens, with his huge size filling the space between the heaven and the earth'"[3]

'Aa'ishah (رضي الله عنها) was asked about the *aayah*,

﴿ثُمَّ دَنَا فَتَدَلَّىٰ ﴿٨﴾﴾

﴾Then he [Jibreel] approached and came closer﴿ *(Qur'an 53:8)*

She said, "That is Jibreel (عليه السلام). He used to come to him in human form, but on this occasion he came in his real form, and he filled the horizons of the sky."[4]

It is narrated in *Ṣaḥeeḥ al-Bukhaari* that 'Abd-Allah ibn Mas'ood said: "Muhammad (ﷺ) saw Jibreel with six hundred wings."[5]

Ibn Mas'ood said concerning the *aayah* –

﴿لَقَدْ رَأَىٰ مِنْ ءَايَٰتِ رَبِّهِ ٱلْكُبْرَىٰٓ ﴿١٨﴾﴾

---

[3] Muslim, 1/159, hadith no. 177.

[4] Muslim, 1/160, hadith no. 177.

[5] Bukhaari, 8/610, hadith no. 4856, 4857.

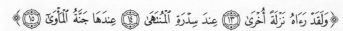

﴾Indeed he [Muhammad] did see of the Greatest Signs, of his Lord [Allah]﴿ *(Qur'an 53:18)* –

"This means green cushions, filling the horizons."[6] These cushions that filled the horizons were what Jibreel was seated upon. Ibn Ḥajar mentioned that An-Nasaa'i and Al-Ḥaakim narrated with their *isnaads* from Ibn Mas'ood that he said, "The Prophet of Allah (ﷺ) saw Jibreel (عليه السلام) with his own eyes, on a cushion which filled the space between heaven and earth."[7]

Ibn Hajar mentioned that Ibn Mas'ood said, according to a report narrated by An-Nasaa'i: "Muhammad (ﷺ) saw Jibreel with six hundred wings, filling the horizon."[8]

In *Musnad al-Imam Aḥmad* it is narrated that 'Abd-Allah ibn Mas'ood said: "The Messenger of Allah (ﷺ) saw Jibreel in his true form. He had six hundred wings, each of which filled the horizon, and there were multi-coloured pearls and rubies falling from his wings."

Ibn Katheer said, concerning this hadith, its *isnaad* is *jayyid.*[9]

Allah said, describing Jibreel:

﴿إِنَّهُۥ لَقَوْلُ رَسُولٍ كَرِيمٍ ١٩ ذِى قُوَّةٍ عِندَ ذِى ٱلْعَرْشِ مَكِينٍ ٢٠ مُّطَاعٍ ثَمَّ أَمِينٍ ٢١﴾

﴾Verily, this is the Word [this Qur'an brought by] a most honourable messenger [Jibreel (Gabriel)], from Allah to Prophet Muhammad].
Owner of power, [and high rank] with [Allah], the Lord of the Throne,
Obeyed [by the angels in the heavens] and trustworthy.﴿
(Qur'an 81:19-21)

What is meant by the "most honourable messenger" here is Jibreel, and the Lord of the Throne is the Lord of Glory, may He be glorified.

---

[6] Bukhaari, 8/611, hadith no. 4858.

[7] *Fatḥ al-Baari*, 8/611.

[8] *Fatḥ al-Baari*, 8/611.

[9] *Al-Bidaayah wan-Nihaayah*, 1/47.

The great size of the bearers of the Throne

Abu Dawood narrated from Jaabir ibn 'Abd-Allah (رضي الله عنه) that the Messenger of Allah (ﷺ) said: "I have been granted permission to speak to one of the angels of Allah, one of the bearers of the Throne. The distance from his earlobes to his shoulders is the distance of a seven - hundred year journey."[10]

This is also narrated by Ibn Abi Ḥaatim, who said: "... as a bird flies." The editor of *Mishkaat al-Masaabeeḥ* said: its *isnaad* is *ṣaḥeeḥ.*[11]

Ṭabaraani narrated in *Al-Mu'jam al-Awsaṭ* with a *ṣaḥeeḥ isnaad* from Anas that he said: "The Messenger of Allah (ﷺ) said: 'I have been granted permission to speak of an angel, one of the bearers of the Throne. His feet are in the lowest earth and the Throne is resting on his horn. The distance from his earlobe to his shoulder is like that of a bird flying for seven hundred years. That angel says, 'Glory be to You, wherever You are.''"[12]

(3) Their most important physical characteristics

(i) The wings of the angels

The angels have wings, as Allah has informed us. Some of them have two wings, some have three or four, and some have more than that.

﴿ٱلْحَمْدُ لِلَّهِ فَاطِرِ ٱلسَّمَٰوَٰتِ وَٱلْأَرْضِ جَاعِلِ ٱلْمَلَٰٓئِكَةِ رُسُلًا أُو۟لِىٓ أَجْنِحَةٍ مَّثْنَىٰ وَثُلَٰثَ وَرُبَٰعَ ۚ يَزِيدُ فِى ٱلْخَلْقِ مَا يَشَآءُ ۚ إِنَّ ٱللَّهَ عَلَىٰ كُلِّ شَىْءٍ قَدِيرٌ ۝١﴾

﴾All the praises and thanks be to Allah, the [only] Originator [or the (Only) Creator] of the heavens and the earth, Who made the angels messengers with wings, two or three or four. He increases in creation what He wills. Verily, Allah is Able to do all things.﴿

(Qur'an 35:1)

---

[10] *Ṣaḥeeḥ Sunan Abi Dawood*, 3/895, no. 9353.

[11] *Mishkaat al-Maṣaabeeḥ*, 3/121. See also *Silsilat al-Aḥaadeeth aṣ-Ṣaḥeeḥah*, hadith no. 151.

[12] *Ṣaḥeeḥ al-Jaami' aṣ-Ṣagheer*, 3rd edn., 1/208, no. 853.

What is meant by saying that Allah made them with wings is that some of them have two wings, some have three or four, and some have more than that.

We have already mentioned the hadith in which the Messenger (ﷺ) stated that Jibreel has six hundred wings.

(ii) The beauty of the angels

Allah has created them in a noble and beautiful form, as Allah says of Jibreel:

﴿عَلَّمَهُۥ شَدِيدُ ٱلْقُوَىٰ ۝٥ ذُو مِرَّةٍ فَٱسْتَوَىٰ ۝٦﴾

﴿He has been taught [this Qur'an] by one mighty in power [Jibreel (Gabriel)].
One free from any defect in body and mind then he [Jibreel – Gabriel in his real shape as created by Allah] rose and became stable.﴾
(Qur'an 53:5-6)

Ibn 'Abbaas said: 'one free from any defect in body or mind' means one whose appearance is beautiful. Qataadah said: one whose form is tall and beautiful. And it is said that 'one free from any defect in body or mind' means one who is possessed of strength. There is no contradiction between the two views, for he is both strong and of a beautiful appearance.

The idea that angels are beautiful is well-established in people's minds, just as the idea that devils are ugly is also well-established. Hence we see them likening beautiful human beings to angels. Look at what the women said when they saw Yousuf:

﴿فَلَمَّا رَأَيْنَهُۥٓ أَكْبَرْنَهُۥ وَقَطَّعْنَ أَيْدِيَهُنَّ وَقُلْنَ حَٰشَ لِلَّهِ مَا هَٰذَا بَشَرًا إِنْ هَٰذَآ إِلَّا مَلَكٌ كَرِيمٌ ۝٣١﴾

﴿Then, when they saw him, they exalted him [at his beauty] and [in their astonishment] cut their hands. They said: 'How perfect is Allah [or Allah forbid]! No man is this! This is none other than a noble angel!'﴾ *(Qur'an 12:31)*

(iii) Is there any similarity in appearance and form between angels and humans?

Muslim narrated in his *Ṣaḥeeḥ,* and At-Tirmidhi narrated in his *Sunan* from Jaabir (رضي الله عنه) that the Messenger of Allah (ﷺ) said: "The Prophets were shown to me, and I saw Moosa, a man of average build, looking like one of the men of (the tribe of) Shanu'ah. And I saw 'Eesa ibn Maryam, and the person I have seen who most resembles him is 'Urwah ibn Mas'ood. And I saw Ibraaheem, and the one who most resembles him is your Companion (meaning himself). And I saw Jibreel (عليه السلام); the person I have seen who most resembles him is Duḥyah." According to another report: Duḥyah ibn Khaleefah.[13]

Is this a similarity between Jibreel's true form, or the form which Jibreel took when he appeared in human form? Most likely it is the latter, because as we shall see, Jibreel often used to appear in the form of Duḥyah.

(iv) Variations in their physical shape and status

The angels are not all the same in their physical shape and status. Some of the angels have two wings, some have three, and Jibreel has six hundred wings. They vary in their status before their Lord:

﴿وَمَا مِنَّآ إِلَّا لَهُۥ مَقَامٌ مَّعْلُومٌ ﴿١٦٤﴾﴾

﴾And there is not one of us [angels] but has his known place [or position].﴿ *(Qur'an 37:164)*

And Allah said concerning Jibreel:

﴿إِنَّهُۥ لَقَوْلُ رَسُولٍ كَرِيمٍ ﴿١٩﴾ ذِى قُوَّةٍ عِندَ ذِى ٱلْعَرْشِ مَكِينٍ ﴿٢٠﴾﴾

﴾Verily, this is the Word [this Qur'an brought by] a most honourable messenger [Jibreel (Gabriel), from Allah to Prophet Muhammad]. Owner of power, [and high rank] with [Allah], the Lord of the Throne.﴿ *(Qur'an 81:19-20)*

---

[13] Muslim, 1/153, hadith no. 167.

i.e., he has a high status and important rank before Allah.

The best of the angels are those who were present at the battle of Badr. In *Ṣaḥeeḥ al-Bukhaari* it is narrated from Rafaa‘ah ibn Raafi‘ that Jibreel came to the Prophet (ﷺ) and said: “What do you think of the people of Badr among you (i.e., those among you who were present at Badr)?” He said, “They are among the best of the Muslims” or similar words. Jibreel said, “The same is true of the angels who were present at the Badr.”[14]

(v) They cannot be described as being male or female

One of the reasons why the children of Adam go astray when speaking about the worlds of the unseen is because they subject those worlds to human criteria. So we see one of them expressing his amazement, in one of his articles, that Jibreel used to come to the Messenger (ﷺ) a few seconds after a question had been put to the Messenger (ﷺ) that needed a reply from Allah. How could he come at such an extraordinary speed? When light needs millions of light-years in order to reach nearby heavenly bodies.

This poor man did not realize that he is like a mosquito trying to measure the speed of an airplane using its own standards. If he had thought about the matter, he would have realized that the world of the angels has its own standards which are completely different from our human standards.

The *mushrik* Arabs also went astray in this regard, as they used to claim that the angels were female, and they mixed this idea, which is far removed from the truth, with an even greater myth, when they claimed that these females were the daughters of Allah.

The Qur’an refuted them on both counts. It pointed out that they had no sound evidence for their claims, and that this notion was nonsense. It is strange indeed that they attributed daughters to Allah, when they themselves hated daughters; when the news of (the birth of) a baby girl

---

[14] Bukhaari, 7/312, hadith no. 3992.

was brought to any of them, his face would become dark, and he would be filled with inward grief, and he would hide himself from the people because of the evil of that whereof he had been informed (cf. Qur'an 16:58-59). This doomed fellow might even lose his mind and bury the newborn girl alive. Nevertheless, they attributed children to Allah, and claimed that these children were female. In this manner myths grow and take root in the minds of those whom the divine light has not reached.

Listen to these verses which tell of this myth and criticize those who believed in it:

﴿فَٱسْتَفْتِهِمْ أَلِرَبِّكَ ٱلْبَنَاتُ وَلَهُمُ ٱلْبَنُونَ ﴿١٤٩﴾ أَمْ خَلَقْنَا ٱلْمَلَـٰٓئِكَةَ إِنَـٰثًا
وَهُمْ شَـٰهِدُونَ ﴿١٥٠﴾ أَلَآ إِنَّهُم مِّنْ إِفْكِهِمْ لَيَقُولُونَ ﴿١٥١﴾ وَلَدَ ٱللَّهُ وَإِنَّهُمْ
لَكَـٰذِبُونَ ﴿١٥٢﴾ أَصْطَفَى ٱلْبَنَاتِ عَلَى ٱلْبَنِينَ ﴿١٥٣﴾ مَا لَكُمْ كَيْفَ تَحْكُمُونَ ﴿١٥٤﴾ أَفَلَا
تَذَكَّرُونَ ﴿١٥٥﴾ أَمْ لَكُمْ سُلْطَـٰنٌ مُّبِينٌ ﴿١٥٦﴾﴾

﴾Now ask them [O Muhammad]: 'Are there [only] daughters for your Lord and sons for them?
Or did We create the angels female while they were witnesses?
Verily, it is of their falsehood that they [Quraysh pagans] say:
'Allah has begotten [offspring – the angels being the daughters of Allah]?' And, verily, they are liars!
Has He [then] chosen daughters rather than sons?
What is the matter with you? How do you decide?
Will you not then remember?
Or is there for you a plain authority?﴿ *(Qur'an 37:149-156)*

Allah will make these words a testimony for which they will be brought to account. One of the greatest of sins is to speak about Allah without knowledge:

﴿وَجَعَلُوا۟ ٱلْمَلَـٰٓئِكَةَ ٱلَّذِينَ هُمْ عِبَـٰدُ ٱلرَّحْمَـٰنِ إِنَـٰثًا ۚ أَشَهِدُوا۟ خَلْقَهُمْ ۚ سَتُكْتَبُ
شَهَـٰدَتُهُمْ وَيُسْـَٔلُونَ ﴿١٩﴾﴾

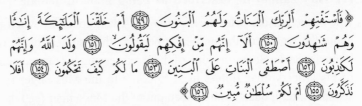

﴾And they make the angels who themselves are slaves of the Most Gracious [Allah] females. Did they witness their creation? Their testimony will be recorded, and they will be questioned!﴾

(Qur'an 43:19)[15]

(vi) They do not eat or drink

We indicated above that the angels cannot be described as being male or female. Similarly, they do not eat or drink the type of food we (humans) eat and drink. Allah has told us that the angels came to Ibraaheem in human form, and he offered them food, but they did not stretch out their hands towards it. He felt afraid of them, but when they told him of their true identity, his fear left him.

﴿هَلْ أَتَىٰكَ حَدِيثُ ضَيْفِ إِبْرَٰهِيمَ ٱلْمُكْرَمِينَ ﴿٢٤﴾ إِذْ دَخَلُوا۟ عَلَيْهِ فَقَالُوا۟ سَلَٰمًا ۖ
قَالَ سَلَٰمٌ قَوْمٌ مُّنكَرُونَ ﴿٢٥﴾ فَرَاغَ إِلَىٰٓ أَهْلِهِۦ فَجَآءَ بِعِجْلٍ سَمِينٍ ﴿٢٦﴾ فَقَرَّبَهُۥٓ
إِلَيْهِمْ قَالَ أَلَا تَأْكُلُونَ ﴿٢٧﴾ فَأَوْجَسَ مِنْهُمْ خِيفَةً ۖ قَالُوا۟ لَا تَخَفْ ۖ وَبَشَّرُوهُ
بِغُلَٰمٍ عَلِيمٍ ﴿٢٨﴾﴾

﴿Has the story reached you, of the honoured guests [three angels; Jibreel (Gabriel) along with another two] of Ibraaheem [Abraham]? When they came in to him and said: '*Salaam,* [peace be upon you]!' He answered: '*Salaam*, [peace be upon you],' and said: 'You are a people unknown to me.'
Then he turned to his household, and brought out a roasted calf [as the property of Ibraaheem [Abraham] was mainly cows].
And placed it before them [saying]: 'Will you not eat?'
Then he conceived fear of them [when they ate not]. They said: 'Fear not.' And they gave him glad tidings of a son having knowledge [about Allah and His religion of True Monotheism].﴾

(Qur'an 51:24-28)

---

[15] Therefore, Muslims should beware of speaking about such matters without knowledge. Those who claim that man originated from animals, monkeys or whatever, should be told the same thing: "Did they witness their creation? Their testimony will be recorded". And Allah says, ﴿I [Allah] made them [*Iblees* and his offspring] not to witness [nor took their help in] the creation of the heavens and the earth and not [even] their own creation.﴾ (Qur'an 18:51)

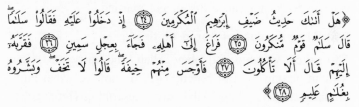

In another *aayah* it says:

﴿فَلَمَّا رَءَآ أَيْدِيَهُمْ لَا تَصِلُ إِلَيْهِ نَكِرَهُمْ وَأَوْجَسَ مِنْهُمْ خِيفَةً قَالُوا۟ لَا تَخَفْ
إِنَّآ أُرْسِلْنَآ إِلَىٰ قَوْمِ لُوطٍ ﴿٧٠﴾﴾

﴾But when he saw their hands went not towards it [the meal], he mistrusted them, and conceived a fear of them. They said: "Fear not, we have been sent against the people of Looṭ [Lot].﴿ *(Qur'an 11:70)*

Suyooṭi narrated from Al-Fakhr ar-Raazi that scholars were agreed that the angels do not eat, drink or get married.[16]

(vii) They do not get bored or tired

The angels worship and obey Allah, and carry out His commands, without getting tired or bored. They do not feel what humans feel of tiredness and boredom. Allah says, describing His angels:

﴿يُسَبِّحُونَ ٱلَّيْلَ وَٱلنَّهَارَ لَا يَفْتُرُونَ ﴿٢٠﴾﴾

﴾They [i.e. the angels] glorify His Praises night and day, [and] they never slacken [to do so].﴿ *(Qur'an 21:20)*

The meaning of 'they never slacken' is they never become weak. In another *aayah* Allah says:

﴿فَٱلَّذِينَ عِندَ رَبِّكَ يُسَبِّحُونَ لَهُۥ بِٱلَّيْلِ وَٱلنَّهَارِ وَهُمْ لَا يَسْـَٔمُونَ ﴿٣٨﴾﴾

﴾Then there are those who are with your Lord [angels] glorify Him night and day, and never are they tired.﴿ *(Qur'an 41:38)*

Suyooṭi inferred that the *aayah* "(and) they never slacken (to do so)" (Qur'an 21:20) means that the angels do not sleep; he narrated this view from Al-Fakhr ar-Raazi.[17]

---

[16] *Al-Ḥabaa'ik fi Akhbaar al-Malaa'ik*, Pp. 264.

[17] *Al-Ḥabaa'ik fi Akhbaar al-Malaa'ik*, Pp. 264.

(viii) The dwelling-place of the angels

The abode and dwelling-place of the angels is in the heavens, as Allah says:

﴿تَكَادُ ٱلسَّمَٰوَٰتُ يَتَفَطَّرْنَ مِن فَوْقِهِنَّ ۚ وَٱلْمَلَٰٓئِكَةُ يُسَبِّحُونَ بِحَمْدِ رَبِّهِمْ ﴿٥﴾﴾

﴾Nearly the heavens might be rent asunder from above them [by His Majesty], and the angels glorify the praises of their Lord.﴿ *(Qur'an 42:5)*

And Allah has described them as being with Him:

﴿فَإِنِ ٱسْتَكْبَرُوا۟ فَٱلَّذِينَ عِندَ رَبِّكَ يُسَبِّحُونَ لَهُۥ بِٱلَّيْلِ وَٱلنَّهَارِ وَهُمْ لَا يَسْـَٔمُونَ ﴿٣٨﴾﴾

﴾But if they are too proud [to do so (i.e., to prostrate to Allah)], then there are those who are with your Lord [angels] glorify Him night and day, and never are they tired.﴿ *(Qur'an 41:38)*

They come down to the earth by the command of Allah, to fulfil the tasks with which they have been entrusted:

﴿وَمَا نَتَنَزَّلُ إِلَّا بِأَمْرِ رَبِّكَ ﴿٦٤﴾﴾

﴾And we [angels] descend not except by the Command of your Lord [O Muhammad].﴿ *(Qur'an 19:64)*

They come down a lot on special occasions, such as *Laylat al-Qadr*:

﴿لَيْلَةُ ٱلْقَدْرِ خَيْرٌ مِّنْ أَلْفِ شَهْرٍ ﴿٣﴾ تَنَزَّلُ ٱلْمَلَٰٓئِكَةُ وَٱلرُّوحُ فِيهَا بِإِذْنِ رَبِّهِم مِّن كُلِّ أَمْرٍ ﴿٤﴾﴾

﴾The Night of *Al-Qadr* [Decree] is better than a thousand months [i.e. worshipping Allah in that night is better than worshipping Him a thousand months, i.e. 83 years and 4 months].
Therein descend the angels and the *Rooḥ* [Jibreel (Gabriel)] by Allah's Permission with all Decrees.﴿ *(Qur'an 97:3-4)*

(ix) The numbers of the angels

The angels are many; no one knows how many they are except the One Who created them:

﴿وَمَا يَعْلَمُ جُنُودَ رَبِّكَ إِلَّا هُوَ ۝٣١﴾

﴿And none can know the hosts of your Lord but He.﴾

(Qur'an 74:31)

If you want to know how many they are, listen to what Jibreel said concerning *Al-Bayt al-Ma'moor* (the Much-Frequented House), when the Messenger (ﷺ) asked him about it, when he reached it on the night of the *Israa' :* This is *Al-Bayt al-Ma'moor*; every day seventy thousand angels pray in it, and they never come back to it."[18]

In *Ṣaḥeeḥ Muslim* it is narrated from 'Abd-Allah that the Messenger of Allah (ﷺ) said: "On that Day, Hell will be brought with seventy thousand ropes, each of which will be pulled by seventy thousand angels."[19] Based on this, those who will bring forth Hell on that Day will be forty-nine million angels.

If you study the texts which have been narrated about the angels who are appointed to take care of each person, you will realize how great their number is. There is an angel who is entrusted with the *nutfah,* two angels appointed to write down the deeds of each person, angels whose task is to protect each person, and an angelic companion *(qareen)* to guide a person.

(x) The names of the angels

The angels have names, but we only know a few of those names. Below are the verses in which some of the names of angels have been mentioned:

---

[18] Bukhaari, 6/103, hadith no. 2207. Muslim, 1/146, hadith no. 162. This version is narrated by Bukhaari.

[19] Muslim, 4/2184, hadith no. 2842.

(a) Jibreel and (b) Mikaa'eel

Allah says:

﴿قُلْ مَن كَانَ عَدُوًّا لِّجِبْرِيلَ فَإِنَّهُۥ نَزَّلَهُۥ عَلَىٰ قَلْبِكَ بِإِذْنِ ٱللَّهِ مُصَدِّقًا لِّمَا بَيْنَ يَدَيْهِ وَهُدًى وَبُشْرَىٰ لِلْمُؤْمِنِينَ ﴿٩٧﴾ مَن كَانَ عَدُوًّا لِّلَّهِ وَمَلَٰٓئِكَتِهِۦ وَرُسُلِهِۦ وَجِبْرِيلَ وَمِيكَىٰلَ فَإِنَّ ٱللَّهَ عَدُوٌّ لِّلْكَٰفِرِينَ ﴿٩٨﴾﴾

﴾Say [O Muhammad]: 'Whoever is an enemy to Jibreel [Gabriel] [let him die in his fury], for indeed he has brought it [this Qur'an] down to your heart by Allah's Permission, confirming what came before it [i.e. the *Tawraat* (Torah) and the *Injeel* (Gospel)] and guidance and glad tidings for the believers.
Whoever is an enemy to Allah, His Angels, His Messengers, Jibreel [Gabriel] and Mikaa'eel [Michael], then verily, Allah is an enemy to the disbelievers.'﴿ *(Qur'an 2:97-98)*

Jibreel is the trustworthy *Rooḥ* mentioned in the *aayah*:

﴿نَزَلَ بِهِ ٱلرُّوحُ ٱلْأَمِينُ ﴿١٩٣﴾ عَلَىٰ قَلْبِكَ لِتَكُونَ مِنَ ٱلْمُنذِرِينَ ﴿١٩٤﴾﴾

﴾Which the trustworthy *Rooḥ* [Jibreel (Gabriel)] has brought down Upon your heart [O Muhammad] that you may be [one] of the warners.﴿ *(Qur'an 26:193-194)*

And he is the *Rooḥ* whom Allah sent to Maryam:

﴿فَأَرْسَلْنَآ إِلَيْهَا رُوحَنَا ﴿١٧﴾﴾

﴾Then We sent to her Our *Rooḥ* [angel Jibreel (Gabriel)].﴿ *(Qur'an 19:17)*

(c) Israafeel

Another of the angels is Israafeel, who will blow the Trumpet.

Jibreel, Mikaa'eel and Israafeel are the angels who were mentioned by the Messenger (ﷺ) in the *du'aa'* with which he opened his prayer at night:

"Allaahumma Rabba Jibreel wa Mikaa'eel wa Israafeel, Faaṭir as-samaawaati wal-arḍ, 'Aalim al-ghaybi wal-shahaadah, anta taḥkumu

bayna 'ibaadika fima kaanu fihi yakhtalifoon, ihdinee lima ukhtulifa fihi min al-ḥaqq bi idhnika, innaka tahdi man tasha' ila ṣiraatim mustaqeem (O Allah, Lord of Jibreel, Mikaa'eel and Israafeel, Creator of the heavens and the earth, Knower of the unseen and the seen, You judge among Your slaves concerning that in which they differ. Guide me by Your Leave with regard to that in which they differ concerning the truth, for You guide whomsoever You will to a straight path)."[20]

(d) Maalik

And among the angels is Maalik, the keeper of Hell:

﴿وَنَادَوْا۟ يَـٰمَـٰلِكُ لِيَقْضِ عَلَيْنَا رَبُّكَ ۖ قَالَ إِنَّكُم مَّـٰكِثُونَ ﴿٧٧﴾﴾

﴿And they will cry: 'O Maalik [Keeper of Hell]! Let your Lord make an end of us.' He will say: 'Verily, you shall abide forever.'﴾ *(Qur'an 43:77)*

(e) Riḍwaan

Ibn Katheer said: "The keeper of Paradise is an angel called Riḍwaan, as is clearly stated in some *aḥaadeeth*."

(f) Munkar and (g) Nakeer

And among the angels whose names were mentioned by the Messenger (ﷺ) are Munkar and Nakeer. They are mentioned in the *aḥaadeeth* which talk about the questioning in the grave.

(h) Haaroot and (i) Maaroot

And among the angels are two whom Allah called Haaroot and Maaroot. Allah says:

﴿وَمَا كَفَرَ سُلَيْمَـٰنُ وَلَـٰكِنَّ ٱلشَّيَـٰطِينَ كَفَرُوا۟ يُعَلِّمُونَ ٱلنَّاسَ ٱلسِّحْرَ وَمَآ أُنزِلَ عَلَى ٱلْمَلَكَيْنِ بِبَابِلَ هَـٰرُوتَ وَمَـٰرُوتَ ۚ وَمَا يُعَلِّمَانِ مِنْ أَحَدٍ حَتَّىٰ يَقُولَآ إِنَّمَا نَحْنُ فِتْنَةٌ فَلَا تَكْفُرْ ﴿١٠٢﴾﴾

[20] Muslim 1/534, hadith no. 770 from 'Aa'ishah *Umm al-Mu'mineen.*

﴿Sulaymaan did not disbelieve, but the *Shayaaṭeen* [devils] disbelieved, teaching men magic and such things that came down at Babylon to the two angels, Haaroot and Maaroot, but neither of these two [angels] taught anyone [such things] till they had said, 'We are for trial, so disbelieve not [by learning this magic from us].'﴾ *(Qur'an 2:102)*

From the context of the *aayah* it is clear that Allah sent them as a test for mankind at some time. Many myths surround them in the books of *Tafseer* and history, for which there is no proof in the Qur'an and Sunnah. It is sufficient to know about them only what is indicated in this verse.

'Azraa'eel

According to some reports, the Angel of Death is called 'Azraa'eel. However, this name is not mentioned in the Qur'an, or in the *ṣaḥeeḥ aḥaadeeth.*[21]

Raqeeb* and *'Ateed

Some scholars mentioned that among the angels are two called *Raqeeb* and *'Ateed*, based on the *aayah,*

﴿إِذْ يَتَلَقَّى ٱلْمُتَلَقِّيَانِ عَنِ ٱلْيَمِينِ وَعَنِ ٱلشِّمَالِ قَعِيدٌ ﴿١٧﴾ مَّا يَلْفِظُ مِن قَوْلٍ إِلَّا لَدَيْهِ رَقِيبٌ عَتِيدٌ ﴿١٨﴾﴾

﴿[Remember] that the two receivers [recording angels] receive [each human being], one sitting on the right and one on the left [to note his or her actions]
Not a word does he [or she] utter but there is a watcher [*raqeeb*] by him ready [*'ateed*] to record it.﴾ *(Qur'an 50:17-18)*

What they mentioned is not correct. The words *raqeeb* (watcher) and *'ateed* (ready) here are adjectives describing the two angels who are always present and witnessing, who are never away from a person. It does not mean that these are the names of the angels.

---

21 *Al-Bidaayah wan-Nihaayah*, 1/50.

(xi) The death of the angels

The angels die just as humans and jinn die. This is stated clearly in the *aayah*:

﴿وَنُفِخَ فِي ٱلصُّورِ فَصَعِقَ مَن فِي ٱلسَّمَٰوَٰتِ وَمَن فِي ٱلۡأَرۡضِ إِلَّا مَن شَآءَ ٱللَّهُۖ ثُمَّ
نُفِخَ فِيهِ أُخۡرَىٰ فَإِذَا هُمۡ قِيَامٞ يَنظُرُونَ ٦٨﴾

﴾And the Trumpet will be blown, and all who are in the heavens and all who are on the earth will swoon away, except him whom Allah wills. Then it will be blown a second time, and behold they will be standing, looking on [waiting].﴿ *(Qur'an 39:68)*

The angels are included in this *aayah,* because they are in the heavens. Ibn Katheer said in his commentary on this verse:

"This is the second Trumpet-blast, the blast which will cause all creatures to fall unconscious. This will cause all living beings in the heavens and on earth to die, except for those whom Allah wills, as is clearly stated in detail in the famous hadith about the Trumpet. Then He will take the souls of those who are left, and the last one to die will be the Angel of Death. Then only the Ever-Living, Self-Sustaining will be left, Who was the First, and Who Alone will be the Last, Everlasting and Eternal. He will say, 'Whose is the Sovereignty today?' three times, then He will answer Himself by saying,

﴿لِلَّهِ ٱلۡوَٰحِدِ ٱلۡقَهَّارِ ١٦﴾

﴾It is Allah's, the One, the Irresistible!﴿ *(Qur'an 40:16).*"

Another verse which indicates that they (the angels) will die is:

﴿كُلُّ شَيۡءٍ هَالِكٌ إِلَّا وَجۡهَهُۥ ٨٨﴾

﴾Everything will perish save His Face.﴿ *(Qur'an 28:88)*

Will any of them die before the Trumpet is blown? We do not know the answer to that, and we cannot discuss it, because there is no text that can give us a positive or a negative answer. Everything will perish save His Face.

2 - ATTRIBUTES

The angels are honourable and obedient

Allah has described the angels as being honourable and obedient:

﴿بِأَيْدِي سَفَرَةٍ ﴿١٥﴾ كِرَامٍ بَرَرَةٍ ﴿١٦﴾﴾

﴿In the hands of scribes [angels].
Honourable and obedient.﴾ *(Qur'an 80:15-16)*

i.e., the Qur'an is in the hands of scribes (*safarah*), i.e., the angels, because they are the emissaries (*sufaraa'*) of Allah to His Messengers and Prophets. Bukhaari said: "*Safarah* refers to the angels. The singular is *saafir. Safartu* means 'I reconciled between them'. So the angels, who bring down the Revelation of Allah are like emissaries who reconcile between the people."[22]

Allah has described these angels as being "honourable and obedient", i.e., He has created them honourable, good and noble. Their actions are obedient, pure and perfect. Hence the one who learns the Qur'an by heart should be one whose actions and words are proper and correct.

Bukhaari narrated that 'Aa'ishah (رضي الله عنها) said: 'The Messenger of Allah (ﷺ) said: 'The one who reads the Qur'an when he knows it by heart is like the honourable scribes and the one who reads the Qur'an and tries his best, and it is hard for him, will have two rewards."[23]

The modesty of the angels

Among the attributes of the angels mentioned by the Messenger (ﷺ) is their modesty. In the hadith narrated by Muslim in his *Ṣaḥeeḥ* from 'Aa'ishah it says that the Messenger of Allah (ﷺ) was lying down in his house with his thigh or his shin uncovered. Abu Bakr asked for permission to come in, and he let him in and spoke with him whilst he was in that state. Then 'Umar sought permission to come in, and he let

---

[22] Bukhaari, 8/691.

[23] Bukhaari, 8/691, hadith no. 4937. Muslim. 1/549, hadith no. 798. This version is narrated by Bukhaari.

him in and spoke with him whilst he was in that state. Then ‘Uthmaan asked for permission to come in, and the Messenger (ﷺ) sat up and rearranged his garment, then he let him come in and spoke with him. When he left, ‘Aa’ishah said: “Abu Bakr came in, and you did not stir or pay too much attention. Then ‘Umar came in, and you did not stir or pay too much attention. Then ‘Uthmaan came in, and you sat up and fixed your garment.” He said, “How could I not feel shy of a man of whom the angels feel shy?”[24]

The phrase “you did not stir” means you did not welcome him warmly.

3 - ABILITIES

(1) Their ability to take on different forms

Allah has given the angels the ability to take on forms different from their own. Allah sent Jibreel to Maryam (Mary) in human form:

﴿وَٱذۡكُرۡ فِي ٱلۡكِتَٰبِ مَرۡيَمَ إِذِ ٱنتَبَذَتۡ مِنۡ أَهۡلِهَا مَكَانٗا شَرۡقِيّٗا ١٦ فَٱتَّخَذَتۡ
مِن دُونِهِمۡ حِجَابٗا فَأَرۡسَلۡنَآ إِلَيۡهَا رُوحَنَا فَتَمَثَّلَ لَهَا بَشَرٗا سَوِيّٗا ١٧ قَالَتۡ إِنِّيٓ
أَعُوذُ بِٱلرَّحۡمَٰنِ مِنكَ إِن كُنتَ تَقِيّٗا ١٨ قَالَ إِنَّمَآ أَنَا۠ رَسُولُ رَبِّكِ لِأَهَبَ لَكِ
غُلَٰمٗا زَكِيّٗا ١٩﴾

﴿And; mention in the Book [the Qur’an, O Muhammad, the story of] Maryam [Mary], when she withdrew in seclusion from her family to a place facing east.
She placed a screen [to screen herself] from them; then We sent to her Our *Rooḥ* [angel Jibreel (Gabriel)], and he appeared before her in the form of a man in all respects.
She said: ‘Verily, I seek refuge with the Most Gracious [Allah] from you, if you do fear Allah.’
[The angel] said: ‘I am only a messenger from your Lord, [to announce] to you the gift of a righteous son.’﴾

(Qur’an 19:16-19)

---

[24] Muslim, 4/1866, hadith no. 2401.

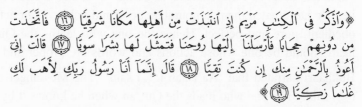

The angels came to Ibraaheem (عليه السلام) in human form, and he did not know that they were angels until they told him who they really were. We have quoted above the *aayaat* which speak of that.

The angels came to the Prophet Looṭ (Lot) in the form of young men with handsome faces and he was grieved on account of them and feared that they may be harmed by his people, for they were an evil people who committed evil actions, and they used to commit sodomy:

﴿وَلَمَّا جَآءَتۡ رُسُلُنَا لُوطٗا سِيٓءَ بِهِمۡ وَضَاقَ بِهِمۡ ذَرۡعٗا وَقَالَ هَٰذَا يَوۡمٌ عَصِيبٞ ٧٧﴾

> ﴿And when Our messengers came to Looṭ [Lot], he was grieved on account of them and felt himself straitened for them [lest the town people should approach them to commit sodomy with them]. He said: 'This is a distressful day.'﴾ *(Qur'an 11:77)*

Ibn Katheer said: "The angels appeared to him in the form of handsome young men as a test and a trial, so that proof might be established against the people of Looṭ, and Allah might seize them with a mighty punishment."[25]

Jibreel used to come to the Messenger (ﷺ) in different forms. Sometimes he came in the form of Duḥyah ibn Khaleefah al-Kalbi (a *Ṣaḥaabi* who was of handsome appearance), and sometimes in the form of a Bedouin.

Many of the *Ṣaḥaabah* saw him when he came in that form.

In *Ṣaḥeeḥayn* (Bukhaari and Muslim) it is narrated that 'Umar ibn al-Khaṭṭaab said:

"Whilst we were sitting with the Messenger of Allah (ﷺ) one day, a man came to us whose clothes were exceedingly white and whose hair was exceedingly black. There were no signs of travel on him and none of us knew him. He sat down in front of the Prophet (ﷺ), with his knees touching his, and put his hands on his thighs, and said, 'O Muhammad, tell me about Islam...'" The hadith states that he asked him about

[25] *Al-Bidaayah wan-Nihaayah*, 1/43.

eemaan (faith), *iḥsaan* and the Hour and its signs.[26]

Then the Messenger (ﷺ) stated that the one who asked these questions was Jibreel, and that he had come to teach the *Ṣaḥaabah* their religion.

'Aa'ishah saw the Messenger (ﷺ) patting the head of Duḥyah al-Kalbi's horse and speaking to him. When she asked him about that, he (ﷺ) said, "That was Jibreel, and he sends *salaam* to you."[27]

The Messenger (ﷺ) told us of a man who killed ninety-nine persons, and when he set out repentant, death came to him when he was half-way to the land to which he was migrating. The angels of mercy and the angels of punishment disputed concerning him, and they referred the matter to an angel who came to them in human form. He (ﷺ) said: "An angel in human form came to them, and they appointed him (to arbitrate) between them. He said, 'Measure the distance between the two lands (the evil place he was leaving and the good place to which he was headed), and whichever one he is closer to is where he belongs.'" No doubt they appointed him as an arbitrator by the command of Allah, and Allah sent this angel to them in human form. The story is narrated in *Ṣaḥeeḥ Muslim*, in *Baab at-Tawbah* (chapter on repentance).[28]

In the story of the three people from among the Children of Israel whom Allah tested, the leper, the bald man and the blind man, we will see that an angel appeared to them in human form.

Some of the scholars indulged in discussions of how the angels change their form from a rational point of view, and they came up with ideas that are of no value. They should not have indulged in this discussion of this matter of the unseen. Allah has told us that the angels may take on

---

[26] Muslim, 1/37, hadith no. 8. Bukhaari from Abu Hurayrah, 1/114, hadith no. 49. This version is narrated by Muslim.

[27] Aḥmad in *Musnad*, Ibn Sa'd in Aṭ-Ṭabaqaat, with a *ḥasan isnaad*. The hadith about Jibreel sending *salaams* to 'Aa'ishah without her seeing him, is narrated by Bukhaari in his *Ṣaḥeeḥ*, 6/305, hadith no. 3217; 7/106, hadith no. 3768.

[28] Muslim, 4/2118, hadith no. 2766.

different forms, but He has not told us how they do so. These scholars should have been content with what the Messenger of Allah and his Companions were content with, and they should have stopped where they stopped. If you want to read some of the discussions on this issue, see the book by Suyooṭi, *Al-Ḥabaa'ik fi Akhbaar al-Malaa'ik.*[29]

(2) Their great speed

The greatest speed known to humans is the speed of light, which is 186,000 miles per second.

But the speed of the angels is greater than that. It cannot be measured by human standards. A questioner would come to the Messenger (ﷺ) and would hardly have finished asking his question before Jibreel would come with the answer from the Lord of Glory, may He be exalted. Today there is no vehicle that can travel at the speed of light, and it would take millions of light years to reach some of the stars that exist in the horizons of this vast universe.

(3) Their knowledge

The angels have great knowledge that they have been taught by Allah, but they do not have the ability that man has been given, to find out about things:

﴿وَعَلَّمَ ءَادَمَ ٱلْأَسْمَآءَ كُلَّهَا ثُمَّ عَرَضَهُمْ عَلَى ٱلْمَلَٰٓئِكَةِ فَقَالَ أَنۢبِـُٔونِى بِأَسْمَآءِ
هَٰٓؤُلَآءِ إِن كُنتُمْ صَٰدِقِينَ ﴿٣١﴾ قَالُوا۟ سُبْحَٰنَكَ لَا عِلْمَ لَنَآ إِلَّا مَا عَلَّمْتَنَآ إِنَّكَ
أَنتَ ٱلْعَلِيمُ ٱلْحَكِيمُ ﴿٣٢﴾﴾

﴿And He taught Adam all the names [of everything], then He showed them to the angels and said, 'Tell Me the names of these if you are truthful.'

They [angels] said: 'Glory is to You, we have no knowledge except what you have taught us. Verily, it is You, the All-Knower, the All-Wise.'﴾ *(Qur'an 2:31-32)*

---

[29] Pp. 261.

Man is distinguished by his ability to find out about things, and to discover the laws of the universe. The angels know that because they learn it directly from Allah. But what Allah teaches them is far more than what man knows. Among the knowledge that they have been given is the knowledge of writing:

﴿وَإِنَّ عَلَيْكُمْ لَحَٰفِظِينَ ﴿١٠﴾ كِرَامًا كَٰتِبِينَ ﴿١١﴾ يَعْلَمُونَ مَا تَفْعَلُونَ ﴿١٢﴾﴾

> ﴿But verily, over you [are appointed angels in charge of mankind] to watch you,
> *Kiraaman* [Honourable] *Kaatibeen* – writing down [your deeds],
> They know all that you do.﴾ *(Qur'an 82:10-12)*

We will discuss this in more detail under the heading of *The Angels and Man*.

The dispute of the hosts on high

The angels discuss amongst themselves matters of the revelation of their Lord which are not clear to them. In *Sunan at-Tirmidhi* and *Musnad Aḥmad* it is narrated from Ibn 'Abbaas that the Messenger (ﷺ) said: "Last night my Lord – may He be blessed and exalted – came to me in the most beautiful form – he (the narrator) said: I think he said, in a dream – and He said: 'O Muhammad, do you know what the hosts on high dispute about?' I said, 'No.' He put His hand (on my back), between my shoulders, until I could feel its coolness on my chest, and I knew what was in the heavens and what was on earth.

Then He said, 'O Muhammad, do you know what the hosts on high dispute about?' I said, 'Yes, about expiations and actions that raise a person's status. The expiations are staying in the mosque after the prayer, walking on foot to join congregational prayers and doing *wuḍoo'* properly at the time of hardship; and the actions that raise a person's status are spreading *salaam*, feeding people, and praying at night when people are asleep.'

He said, 'You have spoken the truth, Whoever does that will live in goodness and die in peace, and he will be free from any sin, as pure as a newborn baby.'

He said, 'O Muhammad, when you pray, say, *"Allahumma inni as'aluka fal al-khayraat wa tark al-munkaraat, wa ḥubb al-masaakeen, wa an taghfir li, wa tarḥamni, wa tatoob 'alaaya, wa idha aradta bi 'ibaadika fitnah, fa'qbidni ilayka ghayr maftoon* [O Allah, I ask you for good deeds, avoidance of evil deeds, and love for the poor. (I ask You) to forgive me and to have mercy on me, and to accept my repentance. If You want to test Your slaves, then take me to You (i.e., cause me to die) without being tested]."[30]

Ibn Katheer said, after quoting this hadith: "This is the famous hadith about the dream. Whoever thinks it happened when the Prophet (ﷺ) was awake is mistaken. It is narrated with different *isnaads* in *As-Sunan*. This hadith is also narrated by At-Tirmidhi from Jahdam ibn 'Abd-Allah al-Yamaami.

Al-Ḥasan said: (it is) *ṣaḥeeḥ*. This dispute is not the dispute mentioned in the Qur'an, where Allah says:

﴿مَا كَانَ لِيَ مِنْ عِلْمٍۭ بِٱلْمَلَإِ ٱلْأَعْلَىٰٓ إِذْ يَخْتَصِمُونَ ﴿٦٩﴾ إِن يُوحَىٰٓ إِلَيَّ إِلَّآ أَنَّمَآ أَنَا۠ نَذِيرٌ مُّبِينٌ ﴿٧٠﴾﴾

﴾I had no knowledge of the chiefs [angels] on high when they were disputing and discussing [about the creation of Adam].
Only this has been revealed to me, that I am a plain warner.'﴿
(Qur'an 38:69-70)

The dispute mentioned in the hadith has been explained by the Messenger (ﷺ).

With regard to the dispute mentioned in the Qur'an, it is explained in the following *aayaat*:

---

30 *Ṣaḥeeḥ Sunan at-Tirmidhi*, 3/9, no. 2580, 2581.

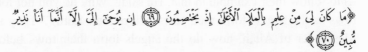

﴿إِذْ قَالَ رَبُّكَ لِلْمَلَـٰٓئِكَةِ إِنِّى خَـٰلِقٌۢ بَشَرًا مِّن طِينٍ ﴿٧١﴾ فَإِذَا سَوَّيْتُهُۥ وَنَفَخْتُ فِيهِ مِن
رُّوحِى فَقَعُوا۟ لَهُۥ سَـٰجِدِينَ ﴿٧٢﴾ فَسَجَدَ ٱلْمَلَـٰٓئِكَةُ كُلُّهُمْ أَجْمَعُونَ ﴿٧٣﴾ إِلَّآ إِبْلِيسَ
ٱسْتَكْبَرَ وَكَانَ مِنَ ٱلْكَـٰفِرِينَ ﴿٧٤﴾﴾

﴿[Remember] when your Lord said to the angels: 'Truly, I am going to create man from clay.
So when I have fashioned him and breathed into him [his] soul created by Me, then you fall down prostrate to him.'
So the angels prostrated themselves, all of them,
Except *Iblees* [Satan], he was proud and was one of the disbelievers.﴾ *(Qur'an 38:71-74)*

The dispute mentioned in the Qur'an was concerning Adam (عليه السلام) and the refusal of *Iblees* to prostrate to him, and how he (*Iblees*) argued with his Lord concerning His preferring Adam over him."[31]

(4) They are disciplined and organized in all their affairs

The angels are disciplined in their worship. The Messenger (ﷺ) urged us to follow their example in that. He said, "Why do you not form your rows as the angels form their rows before their Lord?" They said, "O Messenger of Allah, how do the angels form their rows before their Lord?" He said, "They complete the rows and do not leave any gaps."[32]

On the Day of Resurrection, they will come in organized ranks:

﴿وَجَآءَ رَبُّكَ وَٱلْمَلَكُ صَفًّا صَفًّا ﴿٢٢﴾﴾

﴿And your Lord comes with the angels in rows.﴾ *(Qur'an 89:22)*

And they will stand in rows before Allah:

---

[31] See *Tafseer Ibn Katheer*, 6/73-74.

[32] Muslim, 1/322. hadith no. 430.

﴿يَوْمَ يَقُومُ ٱلرُّوحُ وَٱلْمَلَـٰٓئِكَةُ صَفًّا ۖ لَّا يَتَكَلَّمُونَ إِلَّا مَنْ أَذِنَ لَهُ ٱلرَّحْمَـٰنُ وَقَالَ صَوَابًا ﴿٣٨﴾﴾

﴿The Day that *Ar-Rooḥ* [Jibreel (Gabriel), or another angel] and the angels will stand forth in rows, they will not speak except him whom the Most Gracious [Allah] allows, and he will speak what is right.﴾ *(Qur'an 78:38)*

Ar-Rooḥ here refers to Jibreel.

Look at how precisely they carry out commands. In *Ṣaḥeeḥ Muslim* and *Musnad Aḥmad* it is narrated from Anas (ﷺ) that the Prophet (ﷺ) said: "I will come to the gate of Paradise and ask for it to be opened. The gatekeeper will say, 'Who are you?' I will say, 'Muhammad.' He will say, 'I was commanded not to open it for anyone before you.'"[33]

We may note how precisely they carry out commands by looking at the hadith about the *Israa'*. When Jibreel asked for permission to enter each of the heavens, it was not opened for him until after it was found out who was seeking admission.

(5) The infallibility of the angels

Suyooṭi narrated from Al-Qaaḍi 'Iyaaḍ that "Muslims are unanimously agreed that the angels are virtuous believers, and the Imaams of the Muslims are agreed that our belief about the messengers among them is like our belief about the Prophets with regard to their infallibility in the issues which we have referred to above, and that their responsibilities towards the Prophets are like the responsibilities of the Prophets towards their nations."

Some scholars differed concerning the angels who are not messengers. Some were of the view that all the angels are infallible in the sense that they do not commit sin, based on the *aayaat*:

---

[33] Muslim, 1/188, hadith no. 197.

﴿يَٰٓأَيُّهَا ٱلَّذِينَ ءَامَنُواْ قُوٓاْ أَنفُسَكُمۡ وَأَهۡلِيكُمۡ نَارٗا وَقُودُهَا ٱلنَّاسُ وَٱلۡحِجَارَةُ عَلَيۡهَا مَلَٰٓئِكَةٌ غِلَاظٞ شِدَادٞ لَّا يَعۡصُونَ ٱللَّهَ مَآ أَمَرَهُمۡ وَيَفۡعَلُونَ مَا يُؤۡمَرُونَ ٦﴾

﴾O you who believe! Ward off yourselves and your families against a Fire [Hell] whose fuel is men and stones, over which are [appointed] angels stern [and] severe, who disobey not, [from executing] the Commands they receive from Allah, but do that which they are commanded.﴿

(Qur'an 66:6)

﴿وَمَا مِنَّآ إِلَّا لَهُۥ مَقَامٞ مَّعۡلُومٞ ١٦٤ وَإِنَّا لَنَحۡنُ ٱلصَّآفُّونَ ١٦٥ وَإِنَّا لَنَحۡنُ ٱلۡمُسَبِّحُونَ ١٦٦﴾

﴾And there is not one of us [angels] but has his known place [or position];

And verily, we [angels], we stand in rows [for the prayers as you Muslims stand in rows for your prayers];

And verily, we [angels], indeed are those who glorify [Allah's Praises, i.e. perform prayers].﴿ *(Qur'an 37:164-166)*

﴿وَمَنۡ عِندَهُۥ لَا يَسۡتَكۡبِرُونَ عَنۡ عِبَادَتِهِۦ وَلَا يَسۡتَحۡسِرُونَ ١٩ يُسَبِّحُونَ ٱلَّيۡلَ وَٱلنَّهَارَ لَا يَفۡتُرُونَ ٢٠﴾

﴾To Him belongs whosoever is in the heavens and on earth. And those who are near Him [i.e. the angels] are not too proud to worship Him, nor are they weary [of His worship].

They [i.e. the angels] glorify His Praises night and day, [and] they never slacken [to do so].﴿ *(Qur'an 21:19-20)*

﴿بِأَيۡدِي سَفَرَةٖ ١٥ كِرَامِۭ بَرَرَةٖ ١٦﴾

﴾In the hands of scribes [angels].

Honourable and obedient.﴿ *(Qur'an 80:15-16)*

﴿لَّا يَمَسُّهُۥٓ إِلَّا ٱلۡمُطَهَّرُونَ ٧٩﴾

﴾Which [that Book with Allah] none can touch but the purified [i.e. the angels].﴿ *(Qur'an 56:79)*

And there are many similar reports.

Another group was of the view that this applies only to the messengers among them and those who are close to Allah, and they cited as evidence the story of Haaroot and Maaroot, and the story of *Iblees*. The correct view is that all of them are infallible and that we should think of all of them as being above anything that could undermine their position and high status.

He said: "The answer to the story of Haaroot and Maaroot is that there is no report, sound or otherwise, about that from the Messenger of Allah (ﷺ). Concerning the story of *Iblees,* most scholars deny that he was one of the angels, and they say that he is the father of the jinn, as Adam is the father of mankind.?[34]

This issue was discussed by Aṣ-Ṣafawi al-Armawi, as quoted from him by Suyooṭi. He said: "The angels are infallible, and the evidence for that is as follows:

(i) Allah says concerning them:

﴿وَيَفْعَلُونَ مَا يُؤْمَرُونَ ﴿٦﴾﴾

﴿[They] do that which they are commanded.﴾ *(Qur'an 66:6)*

﴿وَهُم بِأَمْرِهِۦ يَعْمَلُونَ ﴿٢٧﴾﴾

﴿And they act on His Command.﴾ *(Qur'an 21:27)*

These two *aayaat* include doing what is commanded and abstaining from what is forbidden, because a prohibition is a command to abstain, from doing something. The context here is that of praising."

(ii) Allah says:

﴿يُسَبِّحُونَ ٱلَّيْلَ وَٱلنَّهَارَ لَا يَفْتُرُونَ ﴿٢٠﴾﴾

﴿They [i.e. the angels] glorify His Praises night and day, [and] they never slacken [to do so].﴾ *(Qur'an 21: 20)*

---

[34] *Al-Ḥabaa'ik min Akhbaar al-Malaa'ik* by Suyooṭi, Pp. 252.

This is an eloquent description of their efforts in worship.

(iii) The angels are messengers of Allah, because Allah says:

﴿جَاعِلِ الْمَلَٰٓئِكَةِ رُسُلًا ﴿١﴾﴾

﴿Who made the angels messengers﴾ *(Qur'an 35:1)*

The angels are infallible, because Allah says, praising them,

﴿اللَّهُ أَعْلَمُ حَيْثُ يَجْعَلُ رِسَالَتَهُۥ ﴿١٢٤﴾﴾

﴿Allah knows best with whom to place His Message.﴾ *(Qur'an 6:124)*

This *aayah* refers to their perfection in their work.[35]

[35] *Al-Ḥabaa'ik min Akhbaar al-Malaa'ik*, Pp. 253.

CHAPTER TWO
THE WORSHIP OF THE ANGELS

A LOOK AT THE NATURE OF THE ANGELS

The angels instinctively worship Allah. They do not have the ability to disobey Him.

﴿مَلَٰٓئِكَةٌ غِلَاظٌ شِدَادٌ لَّا يَعْصُونَ ٱللَّهَ مَآ أَمَرَهُمْ وَيَفْعَلُونَ مَا يُؤْمَرُونَ ۝٦﴾

﴾[They] disobey not, [from executing] the Commands they receive from Allah, but do that which they are commanded.﴿

(Qur'an 66:6)

Their abstaining from sin and doing acts of obedience is part of their nature, and it does not require any effort on their part, because they have no desires (that could prevent them from doing so).

Perhaps this is the reason why a group of scholars said that the angels are not accountable, and that they are not included in the promises (of Paradise) and threats (of Hell).[1]

What we can say is that the angels are not accountable in the same manner as the sons of Adam are, but saying that they are not accountable at all is a view that is to be rejected. They are commanded to worship and obey Allah:

﴿يَخَافُونَ رَبَّهُم مِّن فَوْقِهِمْ وَيَفْعَلُونَ مَا يُؤْمَرُونَ ۩ ۝٥٠﴾

﴾They fear their Lord above them, and they do what they are commanded.﴿ *(Qur'an 16:50)*

This *aayah* shows that they fear their Lord, and this fear is one of the responsibilities enjoined by shari'ah; indeed it is one of the highest forms of *'uboodiyyah* (being a slave of Allah in the fullest sense), as Allah says of the angels:

---

[1] *Lawaami' al-Anwaar al-Bahiyyah,* 2/409.

﴿وَهُم مِّنْ خَشْيَتِهِۦ مُشْفِقُونَ ﴿٢٨﴾﴾

﴾And they stand in awe for fear of Him.﴿ *(Qur'an 21:28)*

THE STATUS OF THE ANGELS

The best manner in which the angels are described is slaves of Allah, but they are honoured slaves. We have already referred to the fact that the claim made by the *mushrikeen* – that the angels were daughters of Allah – is a false one with no element of truth. Allah showed those who believed this as liars, and described the true nature of the angels and their status in more than one place (in the Qur'an). He said:

﴿وَقَالُوا۟ ٱتَّخَذَ ٱلرَّحْمَٰنُ وَلَدًا ۗ سُبْحَٰنَهُۥ ۚ بَلْ عِبَادٌ مُّكْرَمُونَ ﴿٢٦﴾ لَا يَسْبِقُونَهُۥ
بِٱلْقَوْلِ وَهُم بِأَمْرِهِۦ يَعْمَلُونَ ﴿٢٧﴾ يَعْلَمُ مَا بَيْنَ أَيْدِيهِمْ وَمَا خَلْفَهُمْ وَلَا
يَشْفَعُونَ إِلَّا لِمَنِ ٱرْتَضَىٰ وَهُم مِّنْ خَشْيَتِهِۦ مُشْفِقُونَ ﴿٢٨﴾ وَمَن يَقُلْ مِنْهُمْ
إِنِّىٓ إِلَٰهٌ مِّن دُونِهِۦ فَذَٰلِكَ نَجْزِيهِ جَهَنَّمَ ۚ كَذَٰلِكَ نَجْزِى ٱلظَّٰلِمِينَ ﴿٢٩﴾﴾

﴾And they say: 'The Most Gracious [Allah] has begotten a son [or children].' Glory to Him! They [whom they call children of Allah i.e. the angels, 'Eesa son of Maryam, 'Uzayr (Ezra)], are but honoured slaves.
They speak not until He has spoken, and they act on His Command. He knows what is before them, and what is behind them, and they cannot intercede except for him with whom He is pleased. And they stand in awe for fear of Him.
And if any of them should say: 'Verily, I am an *ilaah* [a god] besides Him [Allah],' such a one We should recompense with Hell. Thus We recompense the *Ẓaalimoon* [polytheists and wrongdoers].﴿
(Qur'an 21:26-29)

The angels are slaves who bear all the characteristics of *'uboodiyyah*: they serve Allah and carry out His instructions. The knowledge of Allah encompasses them, and they cannot go beyond what He commands them to do or go against the instructions that are given to them. They are in fear and awe of Allah, and if it so happened that one of them were to overstep the mark, Allah would punish him for his rebellion.

One aspect of the *'uboodiyyah* of the angels is that they do not make suggestions before their Lord, and they do not oppose any of His commands. Rather they do as they are commanded and hasten to respond.

﴿لَا يَسْبِقُونَهُۥ بِٱلْقَوْلِ وَهُم بِأَمْرِهِۦ يَعْمَلُونَ ﴿٢٧﴾﴾

﴾They speak not until He has spoken, and they act on His Command.﴿ *(Qur'an 21:27)*

They do not do anything except that which they are commanded. The command motivates them, and the command makes them stop. In *Ṣaḥeeḥ al-Bukhaari* it is narrated that Ibn 'Abbaas[2] said: the Messenger of Allah (ﷺ) said to Jibreel, "Why do you not visit us more often?" Then the *aayah* was revealed:

﴿وَمَا نَتَنَزَّلُ إِلَّا بِأَمْرِ رَبِّكَ لَهُۥ مَا بَيْنَ أَيْدِينَا وَمَا خَلْفَنَا وَمَا بَيْنَ ذَٰلِكَ وَمَا كَانَ رَبُّكَ نَسِيًّا ﴿٦٤﴾﴾

﴾And we [angels] descend not except by the Command of your Lord [O Muhammad]. To Him belongs what is before us and what is behind us, and what is between those two; and your Lord is never forgetful.﴿ *(Qur'an 19:64)*

Examples of their worship

The angels are slaves of Allah whose responsibility is to worship Him. They fulfil this responsibility and worship Him with the greatest of ease. We will describe here some of the acts of worship done by the angels which Allah and His Messenger (ﷺ) have told us about.

(1) *Tasbeeḥ* (Glorifying Allah)

The angels remember Allah *(dhikr)*, and the greatest *dhikr* is *Tasbeeḥ*. The bearers of the Throne glorify Him, may He be exalted:

---

[2] Bukhaari, 6/305, hadith no. 3218.

﴿ٱلَّذِينَ يَحْمِلُونَ ٱلْعَرْشَ وَمَنْ حَوْلَهُۥ يُسَبِّحُونَ بِحَمْدِ رَبِّهِمْ ۝٧﴾

﴾Those [angels] who bear the Throne [of Allah] and those around it glorify the praises of their Lord.﴿ *(Qur'an 40:7)*

And all the angels glorify Him:

﴿وَٱلْمَلَٰٓئِكَةُ يُسَبِّحُونَ بِحَمْدِ رَبِّهِمْ ۝٥﴾

﴾And the angels glorify the praises of their Lord.﴿ *(Qur'an 42:5)*

They glorify Allah constantly, without ceasing, either at night or during the day:

﴿يُسَبِّحُونَ ٱلَّيْلَ وَٱلنَّهَارَ لَا يَفْتُرُونَ ۝٢٠﴾

﴾They [i.e. the angels] glorify His Praises night and day, [and] they never slacken [to do so].﴿ *(Qur'an 21:20)*

Because they glorify Allah so much, they are indeed those who truly glorify Allah's praises, and they have the right to be proud of that:

﴿وَإِنَّا لَنَحْنُ ٱلصَّآفُّونَ ۝١٦٥ وَإِنَّا لَنَحْنُ ٱلْمُسَبِّحُونَ ۝١٦٦﴾

﴾And verily, we [angels], stand in rows [for the prayers as you Muslims stand in rows for your prayers];
And verily, we [angels], indeed are those who glorify [Allah's Praises, i.e. perform prayers].﴿ *(Qur'an 37:165-166)*

They glorify Allah so much because *Tasbeeḥ* is the greatest form of *dhikr*. Muslim narrated in his *Ṣaḥeeḥ* that Abu Dharr said: "The Messenger of Allah (ﷺ) was asked what kind of *dhikr* is the best. He said: 'That which Allah has chosen for His angels or His slaves: *Subḥaan Allahi wa bi ḥamdihi* (Glory and praise be to Allah).'"[3]

(2) Standing in rows

We have already mentioned the hadith in which the Messenger (ﷺ) urged his Companions to follow the example of the angels in making

[3] Muslim, 4/2093, hadith no. 2731.

straight rows for the prayer: "Why do you not form rows as the angels form rows before their Lord?" When he was asked about how they form rows, he said: "They complete the rows, and do not leave any gaps." This is narrated by Muslim.[4]

In the Qur'an it says of the angels:

﴿وَإِنَّا لَنَحْنُ ٱلصَّآفُّونَ ﴿١٦٥﴾﴾

﴾And verily, we [angels], stand in rows [for the prayers as you Muslims stand in rows for your prayers].﴿ *(Qur'an 37:165)*

They stand, bow and prostrate. In *Mushkil al-Aathaar* by Aṭ-Ṭaḥhaawi, and in *Al-Mu'jam al-Kabeer* by Aṭ-Ṭabaraani, it is narrated that Ḥakeem ibn Ḥuzaam said:

"When the Messenger of Allah (ﷺ) was with his Companions, he said to them, 'Do you not hear what I hear?' They said, 'We do not hear anything.' He said, 'I can hear the creaking of the heavens, and no wonder they creak, for there is not a spot the size of a handspan, but there is an angel on it, prostrating or standing (in worship).'"[5]

(3) Ḥajj

The angels have a Ka'bah in the seventh heaven to which they go on Ḥajj. This Ka'bah is that which Allah called *Al-Bayt al-Ma'moor* (the Much-Frequented House), and swore by it in *Soorat aṭ-Ṭoor*:

﴿وَٱلْبَيْتِ ٱلْمَعْمُورِ ﴿٤﴾﴾

﴾And by *Al-Bayt al Ma'moor* [the house over the heavens parallel to the Ka'bah at Makkah, continuously visited by the angels].﴿ *(Qur'an 52:4)*

Ibn Katheer said in his commentary on this *aayah*: "It is reported in *Al-Ṣaḥeeḥayn* that the Messenger of Allah (ﷺ) said in the hadith about the

---

[4] Muslim, 1/322, hadith no. 430.

[5] Al-Albaani said: it is *ṣaḥeeḥ* according to the conditions of Muslim. *Silsilat al-Aḥaadeeth aṣ-Ṣaḥeehah*, hadith no. 852.

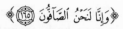

Israa', after he had passed the seventh heaven: 'Then I was taken up to the Much-Frequented House. Every day seventy thousand angels enter it, and they never return to it, and when they leave another seventy thousand come'[6] – i.e., they worship there, and they perform *Ṭawaaf* around it just as the people of this earth perform *Ṭawaaf* around their Ka'bah. The Much-Frequented House is the Ka'bah of the inhabitants of the seventh heaven, hence the Prophet (ﷺ) found Ibraaheem (عليه السلام) leaning back against the Much-Frequented House, because he was the builder of the earthly Ka'bah, and the reward should fit the action."

Ibn Katheer mentioned that the Much-Frequented House is parallel to the Ka'bah, i.e., it is above it, and if it were to fall it would fall on top of it. He said that in each of the heavens there is a House in which its inhabitants worship Allah, and in the direction of which they offer their prayers. The one which is in the first heaven is called *Bayt al-'Izzah* (the House of Glory).

What Ibn Katheer said about the Much-Frequented House being parallel to the Ka'bah is narrated from 'Ali ibn Abi Ṭaalib. Ibn Jareer narrated on the authority of Khaalid ibn 'Ar'arah that a man said to 'Ali (رضي الله عنه), "What is the Much-Frequented House?" He said, "It is a House in the heavens parallel to the Ka'bah. Its sanctity in the heavens is like the sanctity of the Ka'bah on earth. Every day seventy thousand angels enter it, and they never return to it."[7]

Shaykh Naaṣir ad-Deen al-Albaani[8] said concerning this hadith: its men are *thiqaat* apart from Khaalid ibn 'Ar'arah, who is *mastoor*... Then he stated that there is a corroborating *mursal ṣaḥeeḥ* report narrated from Qataadah, who said: "He mentioned to us that one day the Prophet (ﷺ)

---

[6] Bukhaari, 6/103, hadith no. 2207; Muslim, 1/147, hadith no. 162. This version differs somewhat from that narrated in *Aṣ-Ṣaḥeeḥayn*.

[7] Ibn Ḥajar narrated this from Aṭ-Ṭabari and Isḥaaq in *Fatḥ al-Baari*, 6/308, where he spoke at length about its *isnaad*.

[8] *Silsilat al-Aḥaadeeth aṣ-Ṣaḥeeḥah*, 1/236.

said to his Companions, 'Do you know what the Much-Frequented House is?' They said, 'Allah and His Messenger know best.' He said: 'It is a mosque in the heavens, beneath which is the Ka'bah. If it were to fall it would fall on top of it...'"

The editor (Al-Albaani) said: "In conclusion we may note that this phrase (that the Much-Frequented House is parallel to the Ka'bah) is proven when all the *isnaads* are combined."

(4) Their fear of Allah

Because the angels have such a great knowledge of their Lord, their veneration of Him and their fear of Him are very great. Allah says of them:

﴿وَهُم مِّنْ خَشْيَتِهِۦ مُشْفِقُونَ ﴿٢٨﴾﴾

﴾And they stand in awe for fear of Him.﴿ *(Qur'an 21:28)*

How great their fear of their Lord is, is apparent from the hadith narrated by Bukhaari from Abu Hurayrah, who said that the Prophet (ﷺ) said: "When Allah decrees a matter in the heavens, the angels beat their wings in submission to what He has said, (with a sound like) a chain striking a rock."

'Ali and others said:

"The sound reaches them, and when fear is banished from their (angels') hearts, they (angels) say: 'What is it that your Lord has said?' They say: 'The truth. And He is the Most High, the Most Great' (cf. Qur'an 34:23)."[9]

In *Mu'jam aṭ-Ṭabaraani al-Awsaṭ* it is narrated with a *ḥasan isnaad* from Jaabir (رضي الله عنه) that the Messenger of Allah (ﷺ) said: "On the night on which I was taken on the Night Journey (*Israa'*), I passed by the hosts on high, and Jibreel was like a worn mat, from his fear of Allah."[10]

---

[9] Bukhaari, 3/380, hadith no. 4701.

[10] *Ṣaḥeeḥ al-Jaami'*, 5/206.

said to his Companions: "Do you know what the Much-Frequented House is?" They said: "Allah and His Messenger know best." He said: "It is a mosque in the heavens beneath which is the Ka'bah. If it were to fall it would fall on top of it."

The *ḥāfiẓ* (Al-Albani) said: "In conclusion we may note that this phrase (that the Much-Frequented House is parallel to the Ka'bah) is proven when all the *turuq* are combined."[1]

(4) Their fear of Allah

Because the angels have such a great knowledge of their Lord, their veneration of Him and their fear of Him are very great. Allah says of them:

وَهُم مِّنْ خَشْيَتِهِۦ مُشْفِقُونَ

And they stand in awe for fear of Him. (Qur'an 21:28)

How great their fear of their Lord is, is apparent from the hadith narrated by Bukhari from Abu Hurayrah, who said that the Prophet (ﷺ) said: "When Allah decrees a matter in the heavens, the angels beat their wings in submission to what He has said, (with a sound like) a chain striking a rock."

'Ali and others said:

"The sound reaches them, and when fear is banished from their (angels') hearts, they (angels) say: 'What is it that your Lord has said?' They say: 'The truth. And He is the Most High, the Most Great' (cf. Qur'an 34:23)."

In *Al-Mu'jam al-Awsat* by at-Tabarani it is narrated with a *hasan isnad* from Jabir (ﷺ) that the Messenger of Allah (ﷺ) said: "On the night on which I was taken on the Night Journey (*Isra'*), I passed by the hosts on high and Jibreel was like a worn mat, from his fear of Allah."[2]

---

[1] *Bukhari*, 8/520, hadith no. 4701.

[2] *Sahih al-Jami'*, 3/206.

CHAPTER THREE
THE ANGELS AND MAN

1 - THE ANGELS AND ADAM

When Allah wanted to create Adam, He informed His angels of that. They asked Him the reason behind that, because they knew that the sons of Adam would cause corruption and shed blood, and they would disobey Allah and disbelieve. He told them that there were reasons for the creation of Adam which they did not know:

﴿وَإِذْ قَالَ رَبُّكَ لِلْمَلَٰٓئِكَةِ إِنِّى جَاعِلٌ فِى ٱلْأَرْضِ خَلِيفَةً ۖ قَالُوٓا۟ أَتَجْعَلُ فِيهَا مَن يُفْسِدُ فِيهَا وَيَسْفِكُ ٱلدِّمَآءَ وَنَحْنُ نُسَبِّحُ بِحَمْدِكَ وَنُقَدِّسُ لَكَ ۖ قَالَ إِنِّىٓ أَعْلَمُ مَا لَا تَعْلَمُونَ ﴿٣٠﴾﴾

﴿And [remember] when your Lord said to the angels: 'Verily, I am going to place viceroy [mankind] on earth.' They said: 'Will You place therein those who will make mischief therein and shed blood, – while we glorify You with praises and thanks and sanctify You.' He [Allah] said: 'I know that which you know not.'﴾ *(Qur'an 2:30)*

Their prostration to Adam when he was created

Allah commanded His angels to prostrate to Adam when He had completed his creation and breathed his soul into him:

﴿إِذْ قَالَ رَبُّكَ لِلْمَلَٰٓئِكَةِ إِنِّى خَٰلِقٌۢ بَشَرًا مِّن طِينٍ ﴿٧١﴾ فَإِذَا سَوَّيْتُهُۥ وَنَفَخْتُ فِيهِ مِن رُّوحِى فَقَعُوا۟ لَهُۥ سَٰجِدِينَ ﴿٧٢﴾﴾

﴿[Remember] when your Lord said to the angels: 'Truly, I am going to create man from clay.
So when I have fashioned him and breathed into him [his] soul created by Me, then you fall down prostrate to him.'﴾
(Qur'an 38:71-72)

They responded to the command, except for *Iblees*:

﴿فَسَجَدَ ٱلْمَلَٰٓئِكَةُ كُلُّهُمْ أَجْمَعُونَ ۝٧٣ إِلَّآ إِبْلِيسَ ٱسْتَكْبَرَ وَكَانَ مِنَ ٱلْكَٰفِرِينَ ۝٧٤﴾

﴿So the angels prostrated themselves, all of them,
Except *Iblees* [Satan], he was proud and was one of the disbelievers.﴾ *(Qur'an 38:73-74)*[1]

How the angels taught Adam

It is narrated that Abu Hurayrah (ﷺ) said: The Messenger of Allah (ﷺ) said: "Allah created Adam in His image[2], and he was sixty cubits tall. When He had created him, He said, 'Go and greet them – a group of angels who were sitting – and listen to how they respond, for that will be your greeting and the greeting of your descendents.' So he said, *'As-Salaamu 'alaykum* (peace be upon you),' and they said, *'As-Salaamu 'alayka wa raḥmat-Allahi* (peace be upon you, and the mercy of Allah).'" So they added the words *wa raḥmat-Allah.*[3]

The angels washed Adam when he died

When Adam died, his children did not know what they should do with his body, so the angels taught them. In *Mustadrak al-Ḥaakim* and *Mu'jam aṭ-Ṭabaraani al-Awsaṭ,* it is narrated with a *ṣaḥeeḥ isnaad* from Ubayy (ﷺ) that the Prophet (ﷺ) said: "When Adam died, the angels washed his body with water an odd number of times, then they

---

[1] This *aayah* clearly indicates that all the angels prostrated to Adam. This offers a refutation of the view of those who say that those who prostrated were only some of the angels, or that they were only the angels of this earth. The report attributed to Ibn 'Abbaas which says that they were the angels of this earth is *munkar and maqṭoo'* (i.e., it is not a strong report). Ibn Taymiyah stated that the *aayah* is a clear text which is not open to interpretation and it is not permitted to believe the opposite of what is stated in this *aayah*.

[2] In his footnote on this hadith, Dr. Muhammad Muḥsin Khan notes that this means that Adam has been granted life, knowledge, power of understanding etc., which are also attributes of Allah, but that only the names are the same and there is no comparison between the Creator and the created being. See *The Translation of the Meanings of Ṣaḥeeḥ al-Bukhaari*, Vol. 8, Pp. 161. (Translator)

[3] Bukhaari, 11/3, no. 6227. Also narrated by Muslim, 4/2184, hadith no. 2841.

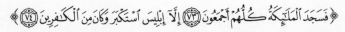

buried him in a grave with a niche (*laḥd*), and said: This is the way of the sons of Adam."[4]

It is narrated in the *ṣaḥeeḥ aḥaadeeth* that the angels washed a *shaheed* from this ummah, Ḥanẓalah ibn Abi 'Aamir, who was martyred in the battle of Uḥud. The Messenger (ﷺ) said to his Companions after Ḥanẓalah was killed: "The angels are washing your companion" – meaning Ḥanẓalah. The *Ṣaḥaabah* asked his wife, and she said that he had gone out when he heard the call to arms, and he was *junub* (in a state of ritual impurity following marital relations). The Messenger of Allah (ﷺ) said, "That is why the angels washed his body."

This is narrated by Al-Ḥaakim and Al-Bayhaqi with a *ḥasan isnaad*. Ibn 'Asaakir stated with a *ṣaḥeeḥ isnaad* that (the tribe of) Al-Aws were proud of the fact that one of their member, Ḥanẓalah ibn Abi 'Aamir, had been washed by the angels.[5]

2 - THE ANGELS AND THE SONS OF ADAM

The connection between the angels and the descendents of Adam is very strong. They are there when a person is created, they guard him/her after he/she emerges into this world. They bring the *waḥy* (revelation) from Allah and they watch over people's actions and behaviour. And they bring a person's soul forth from his body when his appointed time (of death) comes.

(1) Their role in the creation of man

Muslim narrated in his *Ṣaḥeeḥ* that Abu Dharr said: "I heard the Messenger of Allah (ﷺ) say: 'When forty-two nights are passed, Allah sends an angel to the *nutfah* (embryo) and he gives it shape, forming its hearing and sight, its skin, flesh and bones. Then he says: 'O Lord, male or female?' Then your Lord decrees whatever He wills and the angel writes it down.'"[6]

---

[4] *Ṣaḥeeḥ al-Jaami'*, 5/48.

[5] *Silsilat al-Aḥaadeeth aṣ-Ṣaḥeeḥah*, hadith no. 326.

[6] Muslim, 4/2037, hadith no. 2645.

It is narrated that Ibn Mas'ood said: "The Messenger of Allah (ﷺ), who is the most truthful one, told us: 'Each one of you comes together in mother's womb for forty days, then becomes an *'alaqah* (clot) for a similar period of time. Then he becomes a *mudghah* (chewed lump of flesh) for a similar length of time. Then Allah sends an angel to him, who is commanded with four things. It is said to him: Write down his deeds, his provision, and whether he is doomed (destined for Hell) or blessed (destined for Paradise). Then the soul is breathed into him.'"[7]

It is narrated in *Ṣaḥeeḥayn* (Bukhaari and Muslim) from Anas that the Prophet (ﷺ) said: "Allah has appointed an angel over the womb, and he says, 'O Lord, a *nutfah* (mixed discharge from male and female); O Lord, an *'alaqah* (clot); O Lord, a *mudghah* (chewed lump of flesh).' And when Allah wants to decree his creation, he says: 'O Lord, male or female? Doomed or blessed? What is his provision? What is his lifespan?' All of that is written when he is in his mother's womb."[8]

(2) The angels guard the sons of Adam

Allah says:

﴿سَوَآءٌ مِّنكُم مَّنْ أَسَرَّ ٱلْقَوْلَ وَمَن جَهَرَ بِهِۦ وَمَنْ هُوَ مُسْتَخْفٍۭ بِٱلَّيْلِ وَسَارِبٌۢ بِٱلنَّهَارِ ﴿١٠﴾ لَهُۥ مُعَقِّبَٰتٌ مِّنۢ بَيْنِ يَدَيْهِ وَمِنْ خَلْفِهِۦ يَحْفَظُونَهُۥ مِنْ أَمْرِ ٱللَّهِ ﴿١١﴾﴾

﴾It is the same [to Him] whether any of you conceals his speech or declares it openly, whether he be hid by night or goes forth freely by day.

For him [each person], there are angels in succession, before and behind him. They guard him by the Command of Allah.﴿

(Qur'an 13:10-11)

The interpreter of the Qur'an (*turjumaan al-Qur'an*), Ibn 'Abbaas, has explained that the word *Al-Mu'aqqibaat* (translated here as "angels in

---

[7] Bukhaari, 6/303, hadith no. 3208. Also narrated by Muslim, 4/2036, hadith no. 2643.

[8] Bukhaari, 11/477, hadith no. 6595. Also narrated by Muslim, 4/2038, hadith no. 2646. This version is narrated by Bukhaari.

succession") refers to the angels whom Allah appoints to guard a person from before and from behind. Then when the decree of Allah comes, which Allah wills should befall him, they withdraw from him.

Mujaahid said: "There is no person who does not have an angel appointed to protect him when he is asleep and when he is awake, from the jinn, other men and savage beasts. None of these come to him, but the angel tells it, 'Keep away!' except for that which Allah has given permission to befall him."

A man said to 'Ali ibn Abi Ṭaalib, "A group from Muraad want to kill you." He ('Ali) said, "With every man there are angels guarding him from whatever has not been decreed for him. When the decree comes, they move away from him and let it reach him. Your fixed lifespan (decreed by Allah) is a protection for you."[9]

The angels in succession - *Al-Mu'aqqibaat* - mentioned in the *aayah* of *Soorat al-Ra'd* are also those referred to in another *aayah*:

﴿وَهُوَ ٱلْقَاهِرُ فَوْقَ عِبَادِهِۦ ۖ وَيُرْسِلُ عَلَيْكُمْ حَفَظَةً حَتَّىٰٓ إِذَا جَآءَ أَحَدَكُمُ ٱلْمَوْتُ تَوَفَّتْهُ رُسُلُنَا وَهُمْ لَا يُفَرِّطُونَ ﴿٦١﴾﴾

﴿He is the Irresistible [Supreme], over His slaves, and He sends guardians [angels guarding and writing all of one's good and bad deeds] over you, until when death approaches one of you, Our messengers [angel of death and his assistants] take his soul, and they never neglect their duty.﴾ *(Qur'an 6:61)*

These guardians are sent by Allah to protect His slaves until the decreed time of death comes to them.

(3) The emissaries of Allah to His Messengers and Prophets

Allah has told us that Jibreel is the only one who carries out this mission:

﴿قُلْ مَن كَانَ عَدُوًّا لِّجِبْرِيلَ فَإِنَّهُۥ نَزَّلَهُۥ عَلَىٰ قَلْبِكَ بِإِذْنِ ٱللَّهِ مُصَدِّقًا لِّمَا بَيْنَ يَدَيْهِ وَهُدًى وَبُشْرَىٰ لِلْمُؤْمِنِينَ ﴿٩٧﴾﴾

---

[9] *Al-Bidaayah wan-Nihaayah*, 1/54.

> ﴿Say [O Muhammad]: 'Whoever is an enemy to Jibreel [Gabriel] [let him die in his fury], for indeed he has brought it [this Qur'an] down to your heart by Allah's Permission, confirming what came before it [i.e. the *Tawraat* (Torah) and the *Injeel* (Gospel)] and...'﴾
>
> *(Qur'an 2:97)*
>
> ﴿نَزَلَ بِهِ ٱلرُّوحُ ٱلْأَمِينُ ﴿١٩٣﴾ عَلَىٰ قَلْبِكَ لِتَكُونَ مِنَ ٱلْمُنذِرِينَ ﴿١٩٤﴾﴾
>
> ﴿Which the trustworthy *Rooḥ* [Jibreel (Gabriel)] has brought down Upon your heart [O Muhammad] that you may be [one] of the warners.﴾ *(Qur'an 26:193-194)*

Waḥy (revelation) may be brought by angels other than Jibreel, but this happens rarely – as stated in the hadith narrated by Muslim from Ibn 'Abbaas, who said: "Whilst Jibreel was sitting with the Prophet (ﷺ), he heard a creaking sound above him, and he raised his head. He said, 'This is a door in the heaven which has been opened today, and it has never been opened before today, and an angel has come down through it. This is an angel who has come down to the earth, and he never came down before today. He [that angel] gave the greeting of *salaam* and said: Rejoice, for you have been granted two lights which have not been given to any Prophet before you: the Opening of the Book (*Soorat al-Faatiḥah*) and the closing verses of *Soorat al-Baqarah*. You will not read even one letter of them but you will be granted reward.'"[10]

In *At-Taareekh* by Ibn 'Asaakir, it is narrated from Ḥudhayfah that the Messenger of Allah (ﷺ) said: "An angel came to me and greeted me with *salaams* – he came down from the heavens and he had never come down before – and he gave me the glad tidings that Al-Ḥasan and Al-Ḥusayn would be the leaders of the youth of Paradise, and that Faaṭimah would be the leader of the women of Paradise."[11]

In *Musnad Aḥmad* and *Sunan an-Nisaa'i* it is narrated from Ḥudhayfah that the Messenger of Allah (ﷺ) said: "Did you not see what happened

---

[10] Muslim, 1/554, hadith no. 806.

[11] *Ṣaḥeeḥ al-Jaami'*, 1/80.

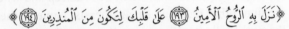

to me just?" They said, 'Yes." He said, "It was one of the angels who had never come down to the earth before tonight. He asked his Lord for permission to greet me, and to tell me that Al-Ḥasan and Al-Ḥusayn will be the leaders of the youth of Paradise, and that Faaṭimah will be the leader of the women of Paradise."[12]

Not everyone to whom an angel comes is a Messenger or a Prophet

Not everyone to whom an angel comes can be counted as a Messenger or a Prophet. This is an illusion. Allah sent Jibreel to Maryam, as He sent him to the mother of Ismaa'eel when she ran out of food and drink. (And it is known that neither of them were Prophetess).

The *Ṣaḥaabah* saw Jibreel in the form of a Bedouin. And Allah sent an angel to that man who visited a brother of his for the sake of Allah, to tell him that Allah loved him because he loved his brother... This happened a lot, and the reason was to make a point.

How did the *Waḥy* (revelation) come to the Messenger (ﷺ)?

It is narrated in Bukhaari from 'Aa'ishah (may Allah be pleased with her) that Al-Ḥaarith ibn Hishaam (رضي الله عنه) asked the Messenger (ﷺ), "O Messenger of Allah, how does the *Waḥy* come to you?"

The Messenger (ﷺ) said: "Sometimes it comes to me like the ringing of a bell, and that is the hardest for me. Then it departs from me, and I understand what has been said. Sometimes the angel comes to me in the form of a man who speaks to me, and I understand what he says."[13]

Jibreel used to come to the Messenger (ﷺ) in his angelic form. This was difficult for the Messenger (ﷺ). At other times Jibreel would change from his angelic form and take on human form, and this was easier for the Messenger (ﷺ).

The Messenger (ﷺ) saw Jibreel twice in the form in which Allah created him:

---

[12] *Musnad Aḥmad*, 5/391; this version is narrated by him. *Ṣaḥeeḥ Sunan an-Nasaa'i*, 3/226, hadith no. 2975.

[13] Bukhaari, 1/18, hadith no. 2.

(i) Three years after the beginning of his (ﷺ) Mission

It is narrated in Bukhaari from Jaabir ibn ‘Abd-Allah that the Messenger of Allah (ﷺ) said: “Whilst I was walking, I heard a voice from the heavens. I raised my head and saw the angel who had come to me in (the cave of) Ḥiraa’, sitting on a throne between the heavens and the earth. I was scared of him, and I went back and said, ‘Cover me!’”[14]

(ii) When he was taken up into the heavens (the *Mi‘raaj*)

These two occasions were mentioned in *Soorat al-Najm*, where Allah says:

﴿عَلَّمَهُۥ شَدِيدُ ٱلْقُوَىٰ (٥) ذُو مِرَّةٍ فَٱسْتَوَىٰ (٦) وَهُوَ بِٱلْأُفُقِ ٱلْأَعْلَىٰ (٧) ثُمَّ دَنَا
فَتَدَلَّىٰ (٨) فَكَانَ قَابَ قَوْسَيْنِ أَوْ أَدْنَىٰ (٩) فَأَوْحَىٰٓ إِلَىٰ عَبْدِهِۦ مَآ أَوْحَىٰ (١٠) مَا
كَذَبَ ٱلْفُؤَادُ مَا رَأَىٰٓ (١١) أَفَتُمَٰرُونَهُۥ عَلَىٰ مَا يَرَىٰ (١٢) وَلَقَدْ رَءَاهُ نَزْلَةً أُخْرَىٰ (١٣)
عِندَ سِدْرَةِ ٱلْمُنتَهَىٰ (١٤) عِندَهَا جَنَّةُ ٱلْمَأْوَىٰٓ (١٥) إِذْ يَغْشَى ٱلسِّدْرَةَ مَا يَغْشَىٰ (١٦) مَا
زَاغَ ٱلْبَصَرُ وَمَا طَغَىٰ (١٧)﴾

﴿He has been taught [this Qur’an] by one mighty in power [Jibreel (Gabriel)].
One free from any defect in body and mind then he [Jibreel – Gabriel in his real shape as created by Allah] rose and became stable.
While he [Jibreel (Gabriel)] was in the highest part of the horizon, [Tafseer Ibn Katheer]
Then he [Jibreel (Gabriel)] approached and came closer,
And was at a distance of two bows’ length or [even] nearer.
So [Allah] revealed to His slave [Muhammad through Jibreel (Gabriel)] whatever He revealed.
The [Prophet’s] heart lied not in what he [Muhammad] saw.
Will you then dispute with him [Muhammad] about what he saw [during the *Mi‘raaj*: (Ascent of the Prophet to the seven heavens)].
And indeed he [Muhammad] saw him [Jibreel (Gabriel)] at a second descent [i.e. another time].

---

[14] Bukhaari, 1/27, hadith no. 4.

Near *Sidrat-ul-Muntaha* [a lote tree of the utmost boundary over the seventh heaven beyond which none can pass].
Near it is the Paradise of Abode.
When that covered the lote tree which did cover it!
The sight [of Prophet Muhammad] turned not aside [right or left], nor it transgressed beyond the limit [ordained for it].﴾

(Qur'an 53:5-17)

The mission of Jibreel is not restricted only to conveying the *Waḥy*

The mission of Jibreel is not restricted only to conveying the *Waḥy* from Allah. He used to come to the Prophet (ﷺ) every year in Ramaḍaan, on every night of that month, to teach him the Qur'an. According to the hadith narrated by Bukhaari in his *Ṣaḥeeḥ* from Ibn 'Abbaas, "The Messenger of Allah (ﷺ) was the most generous of people, and he was at his most in generosity during Ramaḍaan, when he used to meet Jibreel, and he used to meet him every night during Ramaḍaan, to study the Qur'an with him. The Messenger of Allah was more generous in doing good than the wind when it blows."[15]

His leading the Messenger in prayer

Jibreel led the Messenger (ﷺ) in prayer, so that he could learn the prayer as Allah wanted it to be performed. In *Ṣaḥeeḥ al-Bukhaari* and *Sunan an-Nasaa'i* it is narrated from Abu Mas'ood that the Messenger (ﷺ) said: "Jibreel came down and led me in prayer, so I prayed with him, then I prayed with him, then I prayed with him, then I prayed with him, then I prayed with him" – and he counted them off on his fingers five times.[16]

In *As-Sunan* it is narrated from Ibn 'Abbaas that the Messenger (ﷺ) said: "Jibreel led me in prayer at the Ka'bah twice. He led me in praying *Ẓuhr* when the sun had passed its zenith by the length of a sandal-thong, and he led me in praying *'Aṣr* when the shadow of

---

[15] Bukhaari, 1/30, hadith no, 6.

[16] Bukhaari, 6/305, hadith no. 3221. *Ṣaḥeeḥ Sunan an-Nasaa'i*, 1/108, no. 480.

every object was the same length as the object itself. He led me – in praying *Maghrib* – at the time when the fasting person breaks his fast. He led me in praying *'Ishaa'* when the twilight had ended. And he led me in praying *Fajr* at the time when food and drink become *ḥaraam* for the one who is fasting.

On the following day, he led me in praying *Ẓuhr* when the shadow of an object was the same length as the object itself. He led me in praying *'Aṣr* when the shadow of an object was twice as long as the object itself. He led me in praying *Maghrib* at the time when the fasting person breaks his fast. He led me in praying *'Ishaa'* when a third of the night had passed. And he led me in praying *Fajr* when there was a fair amount of light. Then he turned to me and said: 'O Muhammad, these are the times (observed by) the Prophets before you, and the time (for each prayer) is anywhere between these two times (mentioned in each case).'"[17]

The *ruqyah* of Jibreel for the Messenger (ﷺ)

Muslim narrated on the authtority of Abu Sa'eed that Jibreel came to the Prophet (ﷺ) and said, "O Muhammad, are you ill?" He said, "Yes." He said, "In the name of Allah I perform *ruqyah* for you, from everything that is troubling you. From the evil of every living being, or every envious eye, may Allah heal you, in the name of Allah I perform *ruqyah* for you."[18]

Other actions

Among other things, Jibreel fought alongside the Messenger (ﷺ) at Badr and *Al-Khandaq* (the Ditch), and he accompanied the Messenger on the Night Journey (the *Israa'*), etc.

---

[17] *Ṣaḥeeḥ Sunan Abi Dawood*, 1/79, no. 377 - this version is narrated by him. *Ṣaḥeeḥ Sunan at-Tirmidhi*, 1/50, no. 127. *Ṣaḥeeḥ Sunan an-Nasaa'i*, narrating from Abu Hurayrah, 1/109, no. 477.

[18] Muslim, 4/1718, hadith no. 2186.

Why did Allah not send Messengers from among the angels?

Allah did not send Messengers from among the angels because the nature of the angels is different from the nature of man, and so it is not easy for man to be in contact with the angels. It was very difficult for the Prophet (ﷺ) when Jibreel came to him in his angelic form, as we have noted above. When he saw Jibreel in his true form, he was scared, and he went to his wife and said, "Cover me, cover me!"

Because their nature is different, Allah willed that He should send mankind Messengers of their own kind. If the inhabitants of the earth had been angels, He would have sent down to them an angel as a Messenger. Allah, the Exalted, says:

﴿قُل لَّوْ كَانَ فِى ٱلْأَرْضِ مَلَٰٓئِكَةٌ يَمْشُونَ مُطْمَئِنِّينَ لَنَزَّلْنَا عَلَيْهِم مِّنَ ٱلسَّمَآءِ مَلَكًا رَّسُولًا ۝٩٥﴾

﴾Say: 'If there were on the earth, angels walking about in peace and security, We should certainly have sent down for them from the heaven an angel as a Messenger.'﴿ *(Qur'an 17:95)*

Even if we assume that Allah had chosen some of the angels to be His Messengers to mankind, He could not have sent them down in their angelic form. He would have had to make them appear in human form, so that the people could have learned from them:

﴿وَقَالُوا۟ لَوْلَآ أُنزِلَ عَلَيْهِ مَلَكٌ ۖ وَلَوْ أَنزَلْنَا مَلَكًا لَّقُضِىَ ٱلْأَمْرُ ثُمَّ لَا يُنظَرُونَ ۝٨ وَلَوْ جَعَلْنَٰهُ مَلَكًا لَّجَعَلْنَٰهُ رَجُلًا وَلَلَبَسْنَا عَلَيْهِم مَّا يَلْبِسُونَ ۝٩﴾

﴾And they say: 'Why has not an angel been sent down to him?' Had We sent down an angel, the matter would have been judged at once, and no respite would be granted to them.

And had We appointed him an angel, We indeed would have made him a man, and We would have certainly confused them in which they are already confused [i.e. the Message of Prophet Muhammad].﴿ *(Qur'an 6:8-9)*

Allah tells us that the *kaafirs'* demand to see the angels, and to have a Messenger from among the angels come to them, was no more than stubbornness on their part. It was not a request for guidance, and even if it were to happen, they would never believe:

﴿وَلَوْ أَنَّنَا نَزَّلْنَآ إِلَيْهِمُ ٱلْمَلَٰٓئِكَةَ وَكَلَّمَهُمُ ٱلْمَوْتَىٰ وَحَشَرْنَا عَلَيْهِمْ كُلَّ شَىْءٍ قُبُلًا مَّا
كَانُوا۟ لِيُؤْمِنُوٓا۟ إِلَّآ أَن يَشَآءَ ٱللَّهُ وَلَٰكِنَّ أَكْثَرَهُمْ يَجْهَلُونَ ﴿١١١﴾﴾

﴾And even if We had sent down unto them angels, and the dead had spoken unto them, and We had gathered together all things before their very eyes, they would not have believed, unless Allah willed, but most of them behave ignorantly.﴿ *(Qur'an 6:111)*

(4) Stirring up good motives in human hearts

Allah has appointed for each person a *qareen* (constant companion) from among the angels, and another from among the jinn. In *Ṣaḥeeḥ Muslim* it is narrated that Ibn Mas'ood said: "The Messenger of Allah (ﷺ) said: "There is no one among you but there has been appointed for him one *qareen* from among the jinn and another from among the angels." They said, "For you too, O Messenger of Allah?" He said, "For me too, but Allah has helped me against him (the jinn companion) and he has become Muslim, so he does not tell me to do anything but good."[19]

This angelic companion is probably different from the angels who are commanded to record a person's deeds; Allah has appointed him to guide the person.

A person's *qareen* from among the angels and his *qareen* from among the jinn have an influence upon him. The latter tells him and encourages him to do evil, and the former urges and encourages him to do good. It is narrated from Ibn Mas'ood (رضي الله عنه) that the Messenger of Allah (ﷺ) said: "The devil has a hold over the son of Adam, and the angel has a hold over him. The hold of the devil tempts man to do evil and deny the truth. The

---

[19] Muslim, 4/2168, hadith no. 2814.

hold of the angel encourages man to do good and believe in the truth. Whoever experiences anything of this sort, let him know that it is from Allah, and let him praise Allah. Whoever experiences anything of the other, let him seek refuge with Allah from the accursed *Shayṭaan,* then recite:

﴿ٱلشَّيْطَٰنُ يَعِدُكُمُ ٱلْفَقْرَ وَيَأْمُرُكُم بِٱلْفَحْشَآءِ ۖ وَٱللَّهُ يَعِدُكُم مَّغْفِرَةً مِّنْهُ وَفَضْلًا ۗ وَٱللَّهُ وَٰسِعٌ عَلِيمٌ ﴿٢٦٨﴾﴾

﴾*Shayṭaan* [Satan] threatens you with poverty and orders you to commit *Faḥshaa'* [evil deeds, illegal sexual intercourse, sins]; whereas Allah promises you forgiveness from Himself and bounty, and Allah is All-Sufficient for His creatures' needs, All-Knower.﴿"

(Qur'an 2:268)

Ibn Katheer said, after quoting this hadith: "This is how it is narrated by At-Tirmidhi and An-Nasaa'i in the books of *Tafseer* in their *Sunans*, from Hanaad ibn al-Sirri. It is also narrated by Ibn Ḥibbaan in his *Ṣaḥeeḥ*, from Abu Ya'laa al-Moṣuli, also from Hanaad. At-Tirmidhi said: (it is) *ḥasan ghareeb*, and it is the hadith of Abu'l-Aḥwaṣ, i.e., Salaam ibn Saleem..."

Look at the following hadith to see how the jinn-companion and the angel-companion compete with each other to direct a person. Al-Ḥaafiẓ Abu Moosa narrated from Abu az-Zubayr that Jaabir said: "The Messenger of Allah (ﷺ) said: 'When a person goes to bed, an angel and a devil hasten towards him. The angel says, 'End your day with good," and the devil says, "End your day with evil." If he remembers Allah until (sleep) overtakes him, the angel expels the devil and spends the night watching over him.

When he wakes up, an angel and a devil hasten towards him. The angel says, "Start (your day) with good,' and the devil says, 'Start (your day) with evil.' If he says, 'Praise be to Allah who has brought my soul back to life after causing it to die, and has not caused me to die during my sleep. Praise be to Allah Who has detained the souls whom He decreed should die, and has sent back the others until an appointed time. Praise be to Allah Who grasps the heavens and the earth lest they move away from their places, and if they were to move away from their places, there is not one that could grasp them after Him (cf. 35:41), and Praise be to Allah Who holds up the heavens so that they cannot fall on the earth except by His leave,' – then the angel expels the devil and spends the day watching over him."[20]

These *aḥaadeeth* encourage us to do a lot of good deeds in order to reform ourselves, so that the angels come near to us. There is a great deal of good in having the angels near to us. We have mentioned above the hadith of Ibn 'Abbaas, which describes the effect of the Messenger's meeting with Jibreel during the month of Ramaḍaan, to study the Qur'an, and how the Messenger (ﷺ) at that time was "more generous in doing good than the wind when it blows."[21]

(5) Recording the good and bad deeds of the sons of Adam

The angels are appointed to record the deeds of the sons of Adam, both good and bad. These are the angels referred to in the *aayah*:

﴿وَإِنَّ عَلَيْكُمْ لَحَٰفِظِينَ ﴿١٠﴾ كِرَامًا كَٰتِبِينَ ﴿١١﴾ يَعْلَمُونَ مَا تَفْعَلُونَ ﴿١٢﴾﴾

﴿But verily, over you [are appointed angels in charge of mankind] to watch you,
Kiraaman [Honourable] *Kaatibeen* – writing down [your deeds],
They know all that you do.﴾ *(Qur'an 82:10-12)*

For every person, Allah has appointed two angels who are always present and who never leave him; they record in detail all that he does

[20] The editor of *Al-Waabil aṣ-Ṣayyib* said, commenting on this hadith: Something similar is narrated by Ibn Ḥibbaan, no. 2362, Mawaarid, and Al-Ḥaakim, 1/548. Al-Ḥaakim classed it as *ṣaḥeeḥ* and Adh-Dhahabi agreed with him. Its men are *thiqaat*. It is also mentioned by Al-Haythami in *Majma' az-Zawaa'id*, 10/120. He said: it is narrated by Abu Ya'laa, and its men are the men of *ṣaḥeeḥ*, apart from Ibraaheem ash-Shaami, who is *thiqah*. We say the correct name is Ibraaheem ibn al-Ḥajjaaj al-Saami, not Ash-Shaami.

[21] Bukhaari, 1/30, hadith no. 6.

and says:

﴿وَلَقَدْ خَلَقْنَا ٱلْإِنسَـٰنَ وَنَعْلَمُ مَا تُوَسْوِسُ بِهِۦ نَفْسُهُۥ ۖ وَنَحْنُ أَقْرَبُ إِلَيْهِ مِنْ حَبْلِ ٱلْوَرِيدِ ﴿١٦﴾ إِذْ يَتَلَقَّى ٱلْمُتَلَقِّيَانِ عَنِ ٱلْيَمِينِ وَعَنِ ٱلشِّمَالِ قَعِيدٌ ﴿١٧﴾ مَّا يَلْفِظُ مِن قَوْلٍ إِلَّا لَدَيْهِ رَقِيبٌ عَتِيدٌ ﴿١٨﴾﴾

﴾And indeed We have created man, and We know what his ownself whispers to him. And We are nearer to him than his jugular vein [by Our Knowledge].

[Remember] that the two receivers [recording angels] receive [each human being], one sitting on the right and one on the left [to note his or her actions].

Not a word does he [or she] utter but there is a watcher by him ready [to record it].﴿ *(Qur'an 50:16-18)*

The word *qa'eed* (translated here as "sitting") means watching, and *raqeeb 'ateed* [translated here as "a watcher by him ready (to record it)"] means always ready to do that, and he never misses a single word.

The apparent meaning is that the angels who are appointed to watch a person write down everything that he does or says, and they do not leave anything out, because Allah says: ﴾Not a word does he [or she] utter but...﴿

Hence each person will find that his book contains everything that he said or did. When the *kuffaar* see their books of deeds on the Day of Resurrection, they will cry out:

﴿يَـٰوَيْلَتَنَا مَالِ هَـٰذَا ٱلْكِتَـٰبِ لَا يُغَادِرُ صَغِيرَةً وَلَا كَبِيرَةً إِلَّآ أَحْصَىٰهَا ۚ وَوَجَدُوا۟ مَا عَمِلُوا۟ حَاضِرًا ۗ وَلَا يَظْلِمُ رَبُّكَ أَحَدًا ﴿٤٩﴾﴾

﴾'Woe to us! What sort of Book is this that leaves neither a small thing nor a big thing, but has recorded it with numbers!' And they will find all that they did, placed before them, and your Lord treats no one with injustice.﴿ *(Qur'an 18:49)*

In *Ṣaḥeeḥ al-Bukhaari* it is narrated from Abu Hurayrah (رضي الله عنه) that he heard the Messenger of Allah (ﷺ) say: "A person may say something that is pleasing to Allah but he does not realize it, and Allah raises his status by many degrees because of it, and a person may say something that angers Allah, but he does not realize it, and for that he may be thrown deep into Hell."[22]

Ibn Katheer mentioned in his *Tafseer* that Al-Ḥasan al-Baṣri recited this *aayah*:

﴿إِذۡ يَتَلَقَّى ٱلۡمُتَلَقِّيَانِ عَنِ ٱلۡيَمِينِ وَعَنِ ٱلشِّمَالِ قَعِيدٞ ١٧﴾

﴾...One sitting on the right and one on the left...﴿

(Qur'an 50:17)

Then he said: "O son of Adam, the page has been spread out for you (i.e., to record your deeds), and two noble angels have been appointed over you, one on your right and the other on your left. The one on your right records your good deeds, and the one on your left records your bad deeds. So do what you want, less or more. When you die, your book will be rolled up and tied to your neck in your grave, until you emerge on the Day of Resurrection. Then Allah will say:

﴿وَكُلَّ إِنسَٰنٍ أَلۡزَمۡنَٰهُ طَٰٓئِرَهُۥ فِي عُنُقِهِۦۖ وَنُخۡرِجُ لَهُۥ يَوۡمَ ٱلۡقِيَٰمَةِ كِتَٰبٗا يَلۡقَىٰهُ مَنشُورًا ١٣ ٱقۡرَأۡ كِتَٰبَكَ كَفَىٰ بِنَفۡسِكَ ٱلۡيَوۡمَ عَلَيۡكَ حَسِيبٗا ١٤﴾

﴾And We have fastened every man's deeds to his neck, and on the Day of Resurrection, We shall bring out for him a book which he will find wide open.

[It will be said to him]: 'Read your book. You yourself are sufficient as a reckoner against you this Day.'﴿ *(Qur'an 17:13-14)*

Then Al-Ḥasan said: "By Allah, He is being fair towards you, as He will make you a reckoner against yourself."

Ibn Katheer also narrated concerning the *aayah* –

﴿مَّا يَلۡفِظُ مِن قَوۡلٍ إِلَّا لَدَيۡهِ رَقِيبٌ عَتِيدٞ ١٨﴾

﴾Not a word does he [or she] utter but there is a watcher by him ready [to record it].﴿ *(Qur'an 50: 18)* -

---

[22] Bukhaari, 11/308, hadith no. 6478.

that Ibn 'Abbaas said: "Everything that you say, good or bad, is written down. Even when a person says, 'I ate', 'I drank', 'I went,' 'I came,' 'I saw'. Then every Thursday all that a person did or said is examined, and whatever is good or bad is recorded, and the rest is erased. This is what is referred to in the *aayah* where Allah says:

﴿يَمْحُوا اللَّهُ مَا يَشَاءُ وَيُثْبِتُ وَعِندَهُ أُمُّ الْكِتَابِ ﴿٣٩﴾﴾

﴾Allah blots out what He wills and confirms [what He wills]. And with Him is the Mother of the Book [*Al-Lawḥ al-Maḥfooẓ*].﴿

(Qur'an 13:39)

Ibn Katheer mentioned that Imaam Aḥmad used to moan when he was sick. Then he heard that Ṭaawoos said, "Everything is written down, even (a person's) moans." After that, Aḥmad never moaned until he died, may Allah have mercy on him.

The angel on the right records good deeds and that on the left records bad deeds

In *Mu'jam aṭ-Ṭabaraani al-Kabeer* it is narrated with a *ḥasan isnaad* from Abu Umaamah that the Messenger of Allah (ﷺ) said: "The angel on the left holds up his pen (refrains from writing down) for six hours after a Muslim commits a sin. If the person regrets it and asks Allah for forgiveness, he casts it aside (does not write it down), otherwise he writes it down as one (*sayi'ah*)."[23]

Do the angels record deeds of the heart (one's thoughts: good intentions and evil suggestions)?[24]

The commentator on *Aṭ-Ṭaḥḥaawiyyah*[25] stated that the angels do record the actions of the heart on the basis of the *aayah* –

﴿يَعْلَمُونَ مَا تَفْعَلُونَ ﴿١٢﴾﴾

---

[23] *Ṣaḥeeḥ al-Jaami'*, 2/212.

[24] Deeds of the heart, i.e., ideas, feelings and emotions [Translator].

[25] *Sharḥ al-'Aqeedah aṭ-Ṭaḥḥaawiyyah,* Pp. 438.

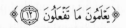

﴾They know all that you do.﴿ *(Qur'an 82: 12)* - which includes both outward and inward deeds.

He also quoted as evidence the hadith narrated by Muslim from Abu Hurayrah, who said: "The Messenger of Allah (ﷺ) said: 'Allah says, 'When My slave intends to do an evil action, do not record it. If he does it, then write it down as one *sayi'ah*. If he intends to do a good deed and does not do it, then write it down as one *ḥasanah*, and if he does it, then write it down as ten''''[26]

According to another hadith whose authenticity is agreed upon by both Bukhaari and Muslim, which is also narrated from Abu Hurayrah, the Messenger of Allah (ﷺ) said: "The angels say, 'O Lord, Your slave wants to do something bad,' although He knows best about him. So Allah says, 'Watch him. If he does it then write it down as it is. If he does not do it, then write it down as one *ḥasanah* for him, for he is abstaining from it because of Me.'''[27]

Question:

It could be asked: doesn't the idea that the angels know what a person is intending to do contradict the *aayah*,

﴿يَعْلَمُ خَآئِنَةَ ٱلْأَعْيُنِ وَمَا تُخْفِى ٱلصُّدُورُ ١٩﴾

﴾Allah knows the fraud of the eyes, and all that the breasts conceal.﴿
(Qur'an 40:19)

The answer is: that this is not one of the matters which is known exclusively to Allah. Even though it is hidden from mankind, and a person does not know what is in his brother's heart, it does not mean that it is hidden from the angels.

It could be said that the angels know some of what is in people's hearts: good intentions and evil suggestions. With regard to other things, such

---

[26] Muslim, 1/117, hadith no. 128.

[27] Muslim, 1/117, hadith no. 129. This version is narrated by him. It is also narrated by Bukhaari, 13/465, hadith no. 7501.

as people's beliefs, there is no evidence that the angels know that.

The angels call people to do good

It is narrated by both Bukhaari and Muslim on the authority of Abu Hurayrah (رضي الله عنه) that the Prophet (ﷺ) said: "No day comes but two angels come down (to the earth) in the morning. One of them says, 'O Allah, compensate the one who spends (for Your sake)' and the other says, 'O Allah, destroy the one who withholds (from spending for Your sake).'"[28]

(6) Testing the sons of Adam

Allah may send some of His angels to try the sons of Adam and put them to the test. In Bukhaari and Muslim it is narrated from Abu Hurayrah (رضي الله عنه) that he heard the Prophet (ﷺ) say: "Allah willed to test three of the Children of Israel – a leper, a bald-headed man and a blind man. So He sent an angel to them.

The angel came to the leper and said, 'What thing do you like most?' He said, 'A good colour and good skin, for the people have a strong aversion to me.' The angel touched him and his illness was cured, and he was given a good colour and beautiful skin. The angel asked him, 'What kind of property do you like best?' He replied, 'Camels (or cows).' [Isḥaaq (the narrator) was not sure; either the leper or the bald-headed man asked for camels and the other asked for cows, or vice versa]. So he (i.e. the leper) was given a she-camel which was ten months pregnant, and the angel said (to him), 'May Allah bless it for you.'

Then the angel went to the bald-headed man and said, 'What thing do you like most?' He said, 'Good hair, and to be rid of this that causes the people to have an aversion to me.' The angel touched him and his illness was cured, and he was given good hair. The angel asked (him), 'What kind of property do you like best?' He replied, 'Cows.' The angel gave him a pregnant cow and said, 'May Allah bless it for you.'

---

[28] Bukhaari, 3/304, hadith no. 1442. Also narrated by Muslim, 2/700, hadith no. 1010.

Then the angel went to the blind man and asked, 'What thing do you like best?' He said, 'For my eyesight to be restored to me, so that I may see the people.' The angel touched his eyes and Allah gave him back his eyesight. The angel asked him, 'What kind of property do you like best?' He replied, 'Sheep.' The angel gave him a pregnant sheep.

Afterwards, all three pregnant animals gave birth to young ones, and multiplied and brought forth so much that one of the (three) men had a herd of camels filling a valley, and one had a herd of cows filling a valley, and one had a flock of sheep filling a valley.

Then the angel came to the leper in the form of a man with leprosy, and said, 'I am a poor man, who has lost all means of completing my journey. So none will satisfy my need except Allah and then you. In the Name of Him Who has given you such a nice colour and beautiful skin, and so much property, I ask you to give me a camel so that I may reach my destination.' The man replied, 'I have many obligations (so I cannot give to you).' The angel said, 'I think I know you; were you not a leper to whom the people had a strong aversion? Weren't you a poor man, and then Allah gave you (all this property).' He replied, '(This is all wrong), I got this property through inheritance from my fore-fathers.' The angel said, 'If you are telling a lie, then may Allah make you as you were before.'

Then the angel came to the bald man in the form of a man who was bald, and said to him the same as he had said to the first one, and he too answered in the same way as the first one did. The angel said, 'If you are telling a lie, then may Allah make you as you were before.'

Then the angel went to the blind man in the form of a man who was blind and said, 'I am a poor man and a traveler, who has lost all means of completing my journey. I have nobody to help me except Allah and then you. I ask you in the Name of Him Who has given you back your eye-sight to give me a sheep, so that with its help, I may complete my journey.' The man said, 'No doubt, I was blind and Allah gave me back my eye-sight, so take anything you wish from my property and leave whatever you wish. By Allah, I will not stop you from taking anything (you need) of my property which you may take for Allah's sake.' The angel replied, 'Keep your property. You (i.e. you three men) have been tested and Allah is pleased with you only and is angry with your two companions.'"[29]

(7) The angels take the soul from the body when the appointed time of death comes

Allah has appointed some of His angels to pull the souls out of people's bodies when their appointed time comes which has been decreed for them by Allah. Allah says:

﴿قُلْ يَتَوَفَّىٰكُم مَّلَكُ ٱلْمَوْتِ ٱلَّذِى وُكِّلَ بِكُمْ ثُمَّ إِلَىٰ رَبِّكُمْ تُرْجَعُونَ ﴿١١﴾﴾

﴿Say: 'The angel of death, who is set over you, will take your souls. Then you shall be brought to your Lord'.﴾ *(Qur'an 32:11)*

There is more than one angel who takes the soul of the dying:

﴿وَهُوَ ٱلْقَاهِرُ فَوْقَ عِبَادِهِۦ ۖ وَيُرْسِلُ عَلَيْكُمْ حَفَظَةً حَتَّىٰٓ إِذَا جَآءَ أَحَدَكُمُ ٱلْمَوْتُ تَوَفَّتْهُ رُسُلُنَا وَهُمْ لَا يُفَرِّطُونَ ﴿٦١﴾ ثُمَّ رُدُّوٓا۟ إِلَى ٱللَّهِ مَوْلَىٰهُمُ ٱلْحَقِّ ۚ أَلَا لَهُ ٱلْحُكْمُ وَهُوَ أَسْرَعُ ٱلْحَـٰسِبِينَ ﴿٦٢﴾﴾

﴿He is the Irresistible [Supreme], over His slaves, and He sends guardians [angels guarding and writing all of one's good and bad deeds] over you, until when death approaches one of you, Our messengers [angel of death and his assistants] take his soul, and they never neglect their duty.

Then they are returned to Allah, their True *Maulaa* [True Master (God), the Just Lord (to reward hem)]. Surely, for Him is the judgement and He is the Swiftest in taking account.﴾

(Qur'an 6:61-62)

---

[29] Bukhaari, 6/500, hadith no. 3464. Also narrated by Muslim, 4/2275, hadith no. 2964. This version is narrated by Muslim.

The angels take the souls of the *kuffaar* and sinners in a harsh and severe manner, with no gentleness or kindness:

﴿وَلَوْ تَرَىٰٓ إِذِ ٱلظَّٰلِمُونَ فِى غَمَرَٰتِ ٱلْمَوْتِ وَٱلْمَلَٰٓئِكَةُ بَاسِطُوٓا۟ أَيْدِيهِمْ أَخْرِجُوٓا۟
أَنفُسَكُمُ ۖ ٱلْيَوْمَ تُجْزَوْنَ عَذَابَ ٱلْهُونِ ﴿٩٣﴾﴾

﴿And if you could but see when the *Zaalimoon* [polytheists and wrongdoers] are in the agonies of death, while the angels are stretching forth their hands [saying]: 'Deliver your souls! This day you shall be recompensed with the torment of degradation.'﴾

(Qur'an 6:93)

﴿وَلَوْ تَرَىٰٓ إِذْ يَتَوَفَّى ٱلَّذِينَ كَفَرُوا۟ ۙ ٱلْمَلَٰٓئِكَةُ يَضْرِبُونَ وُجُوهَهُمْ وَأَدْبَٰرَهُمْ
وَذُوقُوا۟ عَذَابَ ٱلْحَرِيقِ ﴿٥٠﴾﴾

﴿And if you could see when the angels take away the souls of those who disbelieve [at death]; they smite their faces and their backs, [saying]: 'Taste the punishment of the blazing Fire.'﴾

(Qur'an 8:50)

﴿فَكَيْفَ إِذَا تَوَفَّتْهُمُ ٱلْمَلَٰٓئِكَةُ يَضْرِبُونَ وُجُوهَهُمْ وَأَدْبَٰرَهُمْ ﴿٢٧﴾﴾

﴿Then how [will it be] when the angels will take their souls at death, smiting their faces and their backs?﴾ *(Qur'an 47:27)*

But when the angels take the souls of the believers, it is done with kindness and gentleness.

The angels give the believers glad tidings when they take their souls

When death comes to the believing slave, the angels come down to him, give him glad tidings and support him:

﴿إِنَّ ٱلَّذِينَ قَالُوا۟ رَبُّنَا ٱللَّهُ ثُمَّ ٱسْتَقَٰمُوا۟ تَتَنَزَّلُ عَلَيْهِمُ ٱلْمَلَٰٓئِكَةُ أَلَّا
تَخَافُوا۟ وَلَا تَحْزَنُوا۟ وَأَبْشِرُوا۟ بِٱلْجَنَّةِ ٱلَّتِى كُنتُمْ تُوعَدُونَ ﴿٣٠﴾ نَحْنُ أَوْلِيَآؤُكُمْ
فِى ٱلْحَيَوٰةِ ٱلدُّنْيَا وَفِى ٱلْءَاخِرَةِ ۖ وَلَكُمْ فِيهَا مَا تَشْتَهِىٓ أَنفُسُكُمْ وَلَكُمْ
فِيهَا مَا تَدَّعُونَ ﴿٣١﴾﴾

﴿Verily, those who say: "Our Lord is Allah [Alone]," and then they stand firm, on them the angels will descend [at the time of their death] [saying]: 'Fear not, nor grieve! But receive the glad tidings of Paradise which you have been promised!

We have been your friends in the life of this world and are [so] in the Hereafter. Therein you shall have [all] that your inner-selves desire, and therein you shall have [all] for which you ask.'

(Qur'an 41:30-31)

But they give the *kuffaar* the tidings of Hell and the anger of the Compeller (Allah), and they say to them:

$$\text{﴿} أَخْرِجُوٓا۟ أَنفُسَكُمُ ٱلْيَوْمَ تُجْزَوْنَ عَذَابَ ٱلْهُونِ ﴿٩٣﴾ \text{﴾}$$

﴿'Deliver your souls! This day you shall be recompensed with the torment of degradation.'﴾   *(Qur'an 6:93)*

Moosa took out the eye of the Angel of Death

Muslim narrated in his *Ṣaḥeeḥ* that Abu Hurayrah (رضي الله عنه) said: "The Messenger of Allah (ﷺ) said: 'The Angel of Death came to Moosa (عليه السلام) and said, 'Answer your Lord.' And Moosa slapped the Angel of Death in the eye and took out his eye. The Angel went back to Allah and said, 'You sent me to a slave of Yours who does not want to die, and he has took out my eye.' So Allah restored his eye, and said, "Go back to My slave and say, 'Do you want to live? If you want to live, put your hand on the back of a bull, and whatever number of hairs your hand touches, you will live for that number of years.'" (Moosa) said, "Then what?" He said, "Then you die." He said, "Now is better."[30] "The Angel of Death used to come to people face to face, so when he came to Moosa, he slapped him and took out his eye."[31]

Ibn Ḥajar al-'Asqallaani mentioned that some of the followers of *bid'ah* rejected this hadith. In refuting them, he said: "Moosa slapped the Angel

---

[30] Bukhaari, 3/206, hadith no. 1339. Also narrated by Muslim, 4/1843, hadith no. 2373. This version is narrated by Muslim.

[31] This is narrated by Aḥmad in his *Musnad*, and by Aṭ-Ṭabari. See *Fatḥ al-Baari*, 6/442.

of Death, because he saw a man who had entered his house without permission. He did not know that this was the Angel of Death. The shari'ah allows to take out the eye of a person who looks into a Muslim's home without his permission. The angels came to the Prophet Ibraaheem (Abraham) and to the Prophet Looṭ (Lot) in the form of humans and they did not know who they were at first. If Ibraaheem had known, he would not have offered them food, and if Looṭ had known, he would not have feared for them with regard to his people."[32]

Rejecting on purely rational grounds the *ṣaḥeeḥ aḥaadeeth* which speak of the unseen goes against *eemaan* (faith). The first attribute of the pious is that they believe in the unseen, as Allah says at the beginning of *Soorat al-Baqarah* (The Cow). If a report from Allah or from His Messenger is *ṣaḥeeḥ*, then there is no option but to believe it:

﴿وَٱلرَّٰسِخُونَ فِي ٱلۡعِلۡمِ يَقُولُونَ ءَامَنَّا بِهِۦ كُلّٞ مِّنۡ عِندِ رَبِّنَاۗ وَمَا يَذَّكَّرُ إِلَّآ أُوْلُواْ ٱلۡأَلۡبَٰبِ ٧﴾

﴿And those who are firmly grounded in knowledge say: "We believe in it; the whole of it [clear and unclear Verses] are from our Lord." And none receive admonition except men of understanding.﴾

(Qur'an 3:7)

(8) The relationship of the angels with man in the grave, on the Day of Resurrection and in the Hereafter

In our book on belief in the Hereafter we will, *insha Allah*, look at what the angels have to do with mankind after death, such as the two angels – Munkar and Nakeer – questioning a person in his grave. There are angels who bless people in their graves, and others who punish the *kuffaar* (disbelievers) and the sinners (from among the believers). There are angels who will receive the believers on the Day of Resurrection. Israafeel will blow the Trumpet, and other angels will gather the people for the Reckoning. Angels will drive the *kuffaar* to Hell and lead the believers to Paradise. They will punish the *kuffaar* in Hell and will greet the believers with *salaam* in Paradise.

---

[32] *Fatḥ al-Baari*, 6/442.

3 - THE ANGELS AND THE BELIEVERS

In the previous section, we discussed the duties which Allah has enjoined upon the angels with regard to all the sons of Adam, believers and *kuffaar* alike. What we have mentioned about them forming the *nutfah*, protecting people, conveying revelation, accompanying people, writing down people's deeds and taking their souls at death, does not apply only to some of the sons of Adam and not others, or only to believers and not *kuffaar*.

But beyond that the angels play different roles with the believers and the *kuffaar*. We will discuss in more detail the role that they play with each group.

(1) The role of the angels with the believers

(i) Their love for the believers

Bukhaari and Muslim narrated in their *Ṣaḥeeḥs* from Abu Hurayrah (رضي الله عنه) that the Prophet (ﷺ) said: "When Allah loves a peson, He calls to Jibreel and tells him, 'Allah loves so and so, so love him.' Then Jibreel loves him and calls out to the inhabitants of the heavens, 'Allah loves so and so, so love him.' So the inhabitants of the heavens love him, and he will find acceptance on earth."[33]

(ii) Guiding the believers

Bukhaari narrated in his *Ṣaḥeeḥ* from Ḥassaan ibn Thaabit that the Messenger of Allah (ﷺ) prayed for him and said, "O Allah, support him with *Rooḥ al-Qudus.*"[34]

It is also narrated that Abu Hurayrah said: "Sulaymaan (عليه السلام) said, 'Tonight I will go around to one hundred of my women, and each of them will bear a son who will fight for the sake of Allah.' The angel said to him, 'Say, *insha Allah*.' But he did not say it, and he forgot. So he

---

[33] Bukhaari, 6/303, hadith no. 3209. Also narrated by Muslim, 4/2030, hadith no. 2637.

[34] Bukhaari, 6/304.

went around to them (his women) but none of them bore a child, except for one who gave birth to a half formed infant." The Prophet (ﷺ) said: "If he had said *Insha Allah*, he would not have broken his oath and he would have had more hope of fulfilling his need."[35]

The angel was guiding the Prophet of Allah Sulaymaan to the way which is appropriate, correct and more perfect.

(iii) Their sending blessings on the believers

Allah tells us that the angels send blessings on the Messenger (ﷺ):

﴿إِنَّ ٱللَّهَ وَمَلَٰٓئِكَتَهُۥ يُصَلُّونَ عَلَى ٱلنَّبِيِّۚ ﴿٥٦﴾﴾

> ﴾Allah sends His *Ṣalaah* [Graces, Honours, Blessings, Mercy] on the Prophet [Muhammad], and also His angels [ask Allah to bless and forgive him].﴿ *(Qur'an 33:56)*

And they also send blessings on the believers:

﴿هُوَ ٱلَّذِى يُصَلِّى عَلَيْكُمْ وَمَلَٰٓئِكَتُهُۥ لِيُخْرِجَكُم مِّنَ ٱلظُّلُمَٰتِ إِلَى ٱلنُّورِۚ
وَكَانَ بِٱلْمُؤْمِنِينَ رَحِيمًا ﴿٤٣﴾﴾

> ﴾He it is Who sends *Ṣalaah* [His blessings] on you, and His angels too [ask Allah to bless and forgive you], that He may bring you out from darkness [of disbelief and polytheism] into light [of Belief and Islamic Monotheism]. And He is Ever Most Merciful to the believers.﴿ *(Qur'an 33:43)*

Ṣalaah (blessings) from Allah means that He praises His slave before His angels. This is narrated by Bukhaari from Abu'l-'Aaliyah. Someone else said: *Ṣalaah* (blessings) from Allah means mercy. It may be said that

---

[35] Bukhaari, 9/339, hadith no. 5242. Ibn Ḥajar said (*Fatḥ al-Baari*, 6/460) what may be summed up as follows: According to the report of Al-Mugheerah, it was seventy women. According to the report of Shu'ayb in *Al-Aymaan wan-Nudhoor*, it was ninety. The author thought that this was more likely? This is also narrated by Muslim in his *Ṣaḥeeḥ* (3/1276, hadith no. 1654); in one report it says sixty and in the other it says seventy. In a third report it says ninety.

there is no contradiction between the two views.

Ṣalaah (blessings) from the angels means that they pray for people and seek forgiveness for them. This is what we will discuss in more detail below.

Examples of deeds for which the angels send blessings upon a person

(a) Teaching people good things

At-Tirmidhi narrated in his *Sunan* from Abu Umaamah that the Messenger (ﷺ) said: "Allah and His angels, and the inhabitants of the heavens and the earth, even the ant in its hole, and even the fish, send blessings upon the one who teaches the people good things."[36]

(b) Those who wait for prayer in congregation

In *Ṣaḥeeḥ Muslim* it is narrated that Abu Hurayrah said: "The Messenger of Allah (ﷺ) said: 'The angels send blessings on any one of you so long as he stays where he is sitting. They say, 'O Allah, forgive him, O Allah, have mercy on him,' so long as he does not break his *wuḍoo'*.''''[37]

(c) Those who pray in the first row

In *Sunan Abi Dawood* it is narrated from Al-Baraa' ibn 'Aazib (رضي الله عنه) that the Messenger of Allah (ﷺ) said: "Allah and His angels send blessings on the first rows."[38]

In *Sunan an-Nasaa'i* it says: "... on the front rows."[39]

In *Sunan Ibn Maajah* it is narrated from the hadith of Al-Baraa' and the hadith of 'Abd ar-Raḥmaan ibn 'Awf that "Allah and His angels send blessings on the first row."[40]

---

[36] *Ṣaḥeeḥ Sunan at-Tirmidhi*, 2/343, no. 2161.

[37] Bukhaari, 2/131, hadith no. 647. Also narrated by Muslim, 1/459, hadith no. 639. This version is narrated by Muslim.

[38] *Ṣaḥeeḥ Sunan Abi Dawood*, 1/120, no. 618.

[39] *Ṣaḥeeḥ Sunan an-Nasaa'i*, 1/175, no. 781.

[40] *Ṣaḥeeḥ Sunan Ibn Maajah*, 1/164, no. 816.

(d) Those who fill the gaps in the rows

In *Sunan Ibn Maajah* it is narrated that 'Aa'ishah said: "The Messenger of Allah (ﷺ) said: 'Allah and His angels send blessings on those who complete the rows, and whoever fills a gap (in a row), Allah will raise his status because of it.'"[41]

(e) Those who eat *suḥoor*

In *Ṣaheeḥ Ibn Ḥibbaan* and *Mu'jam aṭ-Ṭabaraani al-Awsaṭ* it is narrated with a *ḥasan isnaad* from Ibn 'Umar (may Allah be pleased with them both) that the Messenger of Allah (ﷺ) said: "Allah and His angels send blessings upon those who eat *suḥoor*."[42]

(f) Those who send blessings upon the Prophet (ﷺ)

Aḥmad narrated in his *Musnad* and Al-Diyaa' narrated in *Al-Mukhtaarah* from 'Aamir ibn Rabee'ah with a *ḥasan isnaad* that the Messenger of Allah (ﷺ) said: "There is no person who sends blessings on me, but the angels send blessings on him so long as he sends blessings on me. So let a person do a little of that or a lot."[43]

(g) Those who visit the sick

Abu Dawood narrated from 'Ali ibn Abi Ṭaalib (رضي الله عنه) that the Prophet (ﷺ) said: "There is no man who visits a sick person in the evening, but seventy thousand angels go out with him, and pray for forgiveness for him until the morning, and he will have provision in Paradise. And whoever goes to him in the morning, seventy thousand angels go with him, and they pray for forgiveness for him until the evening, and he will have provision in Paradise."[44]

---

41 *Ṣaheeḥ Sunan Ibn Maajah*, 1/164, no. 814.

42 *Ṣaheeḥ al-Jaami'*, 2/135.

43 *Ṣaheeḥ al-Jaami', 5/174.*

44 *Ṣaheeḥ Sunan Abi Dawood*, 2/598, no. 2655. Abu Dawood stated that it is *ṣaheeḥ marfoo'*, he also narrated a *ṣaheeḥ mawqoof* report from 'Ali.

Does the angels' sending blessings on us have any effect?

Allah, the Almighty, says:

﴿هُوَ ٱلَّذِى يُصَلِّى عَلَيْكُمْ وَمَلَٰٓئِكَتُهُۥ لِيُخْرِجَكُم مِّنَ ٱلظُّلُمَٰتِ إِلَى ٱلنُّورِ ۚ ﴿٤٣﴾﴾

﴾He it is Who sends *Ṣalaah* [His blessings] on you, and His angels too [ask Allah to bless and forgive you], that He may bring you out from darkness [of disbelief and polytheism] into light [of Belief and Islamic Monotheism].﴿ *(Qur'an 33:43)*

This *aayah* tells us that when Allah mentions us to the hosts on high, and when the angels pray for the believers and ask for forgiveness for them, this has the effect of guiding us and ridding us of the darkness of *kufr* and *shirk* and sin, leading us to the light which means the right way and the path of truth, which is Islam. Thus we learn what Allah wants of us, and gives us the light by which we will be guided to righteous words and deeds and people.

(iv) Saying *"Ameen"* to the *du'aa'* of the believers

The angels say *"ameen"* to the *du'aa'* of the believer, thus making the *du'aa'* more likely to be answered. In *Ṣaḥeeḥ Muslim* and *Sunan Ibn Maajah* it is narrated from Abu'd-Dardaa' that the Prophet (ﷺ) said: "The *du'aa'* of a person for his Muslim brother in his absence will be answered. At his head there is an angel, and every time he prays for him for something good, the angel who has been appointed to be with him says, '*Ameen,* and may you have likewise.'"[45]

Because a believer's prayer against himself is very likely to be answered, the believer should not pray against himself. In *Ṣaḥeeḥ Muslim* it is narrated that Umm Salamah said: "The Messenger of Allah (ﷺ) said: 'Do not pray for anything but good for yourselves, for the angels say *"ameen"* to whatever you say.'"[46]

---

[45] Muslim, 4/2094, hadith no. 2733; *Ṣaḥeeḥ Sunan Ibn Maajah*, 2/149, no. 2340. This version is narrated by Muslim.

[46] Muslim, 2/634, hadith no. 920.

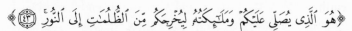

(v) Their prayers for forgiveness for the believers

Allah tells us that the angels pray for forgiveness for those who are on earth:

﴿تَكَادُ ٱلسَّمَٰوَٰتُ يَتَفَطَّرْنَ مِن فَوْقِهِنَّ ۚ وَٱلْمَلَٰٓئِكَةُ يُسَبِّحُونَ بِحَمْدِ رَبِّهِمْ
وَيَسْتَغْفِرُونَ لِمَن فِى ٱلْأَرْضِ ۗ أَلَآ إِنَّ ٱللَّهَ هُوَ ٱلْغَفُورُ ٱلرَّحِيمُ ﴿٥﴾﴾

﴾Nearly the heavens might be rent asunder from above them [by His Majesty], and the angels glorify the praises of their Lord, and ask for forgiveness for those on the earth. Verily, Allah is the Oft-Forgiving, the Most Merciful.﴿ *(Qur'an 42:5)*

In *Soorah Ghaafir*, Allah tells us that the bearers of the Throne and the angels who are around the Throne glorify their Lord and submit themselves to Him, and they pray for forgiveness especially for the believers who repent. They pray that Allah will save them from the Fire and admit them to Paradise, and keep them from committing sins and acts of disobedience:

﴿ٱلَّذِينَ يَحْمِلُونَ ٱلْعَرْشَ وَمَنْ حَوْلَهُۥ يُسَبِّحُونَ بِحَمْدِ رَبِّهِمْ وَيُؤْمِنُونَ بِهِۦ وَيَسْتَغْفِرُونَ
لِلَّذِينَ ءَامَنُوا۟ ۖ رَبَّنَا وَسِعْتَ كُلَّ شَىْءٍ رَّحْمَةً وَعِلْمًا فَٱغْفِرْ لِلَّذِينَ تَابُوا۟
وَٱتَّبَعُوا۟ سَبِيلَكَ وَقِهِمْ عَذَابَ ٱلْجَحِيمِ ﴿٧﴾ رَبَّنَا وَأَدْخِلْهُمْ جَنَّٰتِ عَدْنٍ ٱلَّتِى
وَعَدتَّهُمْ وَمَن صَلَحَ مِنْ ءَابَآئِهِمْ وَأَزْوَٰجِهِمْ وَذُرِّيَّٰتِهِمْ ۚ إِنَّكَ أَنتَ ٱلْعَزِيزُ
ٱلْحَكِيمُ ﴿٨﴾ وَقِهِمُ ٱلسَّيِّـَٔاتِ ۚ وَمَن تَقِ ٱلسَّيِّـَٔاتِ يَوْمَئِذٍ فَقَدْ رَحِمْتَهُۥ ۚ
وَذَٰلِكَ هُوَ ٱلْفَوْزُ ٱلْعَظِيمُ ﴿٩﴾﴾

﴾Those [angels] who bear the Throne [of Allah] and those around it glorify the praises of their Lord, and believe in Him, and ask forgiveness for those who believe [in the Oneness of Allah] [saying]: 'Our Lord! You comprehend all things in mercy and knowledge, so forgive those who repent and follow Your way, and save them from the torment of the blazing Fire!

Our Lord! And make them enter the *'Adn* [Eden] Paradise [everlasting Gardens] which you have promised them – and to the righteous among their fathers, their wives, and their offspring!

> Verily, You are the All-Mighty, the All-Wise.
> And save them from [the punishment for what they did of] the sins, and whomsoever You save from [the punishment for what he did of] the sins [i.e. pardon him] that Day, him verily, You have taken into mercy.' And that is the supreme success.﴾ *(Qur'an 40:7-9)*

(vi) They attend gatherings of knowledge and circles of *dhikr,* and surround those present with their wings

In *Ṣaḥeeḥ al-Bukhaari* and *Ṣaḥeeḥ Muslim* it is narrated that Abu Hurayrah (رضي الله عنه) said: "The Messenger of Allah (ﷺ) said: 'Allah has angels who go around the highways and byways, seeking out the people of *dhikr*. If they find some people who are remembering Allah, they call out, 'Come to what you are looking for!' And they encompass them with their wings up to the first heaven.'"[47]

In *Ṣaḥeeḥ Muslim* it is narrated that Abu Hurayrah (رضي الله عنه) said: "The Messenger of Allah (ﷺ) said: 'No people gather in one of the houses of Allah to recite the Book of Allah and teach it to one another, but tranquillity descends upon them, mercy overshadows them and the angels surround them, and Allah mentions them to those who are with Him.'"[48]

In *Sunan at-Tirmidhi* it is narrated that Abu'd-Dardaa' said: "I heard the Messenger of Allah (ﷺ) say, 'The angels extend their wings (out of humbleness) towards the seeker of knowledge, because they are pleased with what he is doing.'"[49]

Righteous deeds, as you can see, bring the angels closer to us and bring us closer to them. If people were able to maintain a high spiritual state they would reach the level of actually seeing the angels and shaking hands with them, as is in the hadith narrated by Muslim from Ḥanẓalah al-Usaydi (رضي الله عنه) who said that the Prophet (ﷺ) said:

---

[47] Bukhaari, 11/208, hadith no. 6408. Also narrated by Muslim, 4/2069, hadith no. 2689. This version is narrated by Bukhaari.

[48] Muslim, 4/2074, hadith no. 2699.

[49] *Ṣaḥeeḥ Sunan at-Tirmidhi*, 2/342, no. 2159.

"By the One in Whose hand is my soul, if you remained in the state in which you are when you are with me, and you continued to remember Allah, the angels would shake hands with you in your beds and on the street."[50]

According to a report narrated by At-Tirmidhi from Ḥanẓalah, he said, "The Messenger of Allah (ﷺ) said: 'If you continued to be as you are with me, the angels would shade you with their wings.'"[51]

(vii) The angels record those who attend *Jumu'ah*

These angels record some of the deeds of people, and they record those who go to Friday prayers in order of attendance. It is narrated that Abu Hurayrah said: "The Messenger of Allah (ﷺ) said: 'When Friday comes, the angels stand at the door of the mosque and write down who comes first. When the Imaam comes out, they close their records and sit down to listen to the *dhikr*." Agreed upon by Bukhaari and Muslim.[52]

They record whatever people say of good things. In *Ṣaḥeeḥ al-Bukhaari* and elsewhere it is narrated that Rifaa'ah ibn Raafi' al-Zarqi said: "One day we were praying behind the Prophet (ﷺ) and when he raised his head from *rukoo'*, he said, *'Sami' Allahu liman ḥamidah* (Allah hears those who praise Him).' A man behind him said, *Rabbanaa wa laka'l-ḥamd ḥamdan katheeran ṭayyiban mubaarakan fihi* (Our Lord, to You be praise, much good and blessed praise).' When he finished the prayer, he said, 'Who was the one who spoke?' The man said, 'Me.' He [the Prophet (ﷺ)] said, 'I saw thirty-odd angels rushing to see which of them would write it down first.'"[53]

These recording angels are definitely other than the two angels who write down a person's good deeds and evil deeds, because they are described as being thirty-odd.

---

[50] Muslim, 4/2106, hadith no. 2750.

[51] *Ṣaḥeeḥ Sunan at-Tirmidhi*, 2/298, no. 1994.

[52] *Mishkaat al-Maṣaabeeḥ*, 1/436, no. 1384.

[53] Bukhaari, 2/284, hadith no. 799.

(vii) The angels come and go among us

These angels who go about in the highways and byways, looking for *dhikr* and witnessing *Jumu'ah* prayers and prayers in *jamaa'ah*, come and go among us. When one group comes another group goes, and they meet at *Fajr* prayer and at *'Aṣr* prayer. In *Ṣaḥeeḥ al-Bukhaari* and *Ṣaḥeeḥ Muslim* it is narrated from Abu Hurayrah (رضي الله عنه) that the Messenger of Allah (ﷺ) said: "Allah has angels who come and go among you, angels at night and angels during the day. They meet at *Fajr* prayer and *'Aṣr* prayer. Then those who had stayed among you ascend and their Lord asks them, although He knows best about them, 'How did you leave My slaves?' They say, 'When we left them they were praying, and when we came to them they were praying.'"[54]

Perhaps these are the ones who take the people's actions up to their Lord. In *Ṣaḥeeḥ Muslim* it is narrated that Abu Moosa al-Ash'ari (رضي الله عنه) said: "The Messenger of Allah (ﷺ) stood up among us and told us five things. He said: 'Allah does not sleep, and it is not befitting that He should sleep. He lowers the scale and lifts it. The deeds of the night are taken up to Him before the deeds of the day, and the deeds of the day before the deeds of the night...'"[55]

Allah has ascribed a high status to *Fajr* prayer, because the angels witness it. He says:

﴿وَقُرْءَانَ ٱلْفَجْرِ ۖ إِنَّ قُرْءَانَ ٱلْفَجْرِ كَانَ مَشْهُودًا ﴿٧٨﴾﴾

> ﴾And recite the Qur'an in the early dawn [i.e. the — *Fajr*— morning prayer]. Verily, the recitation of the Qur'an in the early dawn [i.e. the morning — *Fajr* prayer] is ever witnessed [attended by the angels in charge of mankind of the day and the night].﴿
>
> *(Qur'an 17:78)*

---

[54] Bukhaari, 6/306, hadith no. 3223. Also narrated by Muslim, 1/439, hadith no. 632.

[55] Muslim, 1/162, hadith no. 179. According to another report by Muslim, ...four words...

(ix) They come down when a believer recites the Qur'an

Among the angels are those who come down from heaven when the Qur'an is being read. In *Ṣaḥeeḥ Muslim* it is narrated that Al-Baraa' ibn 'Aazib said: "A man read *Soorat al-Kahf*, and in the house there was an animal. It began to act nervously, (so he checked on it and saw that) there was a mist or a cloud above it. He mentioned that to the Prophet (ﷺ) and he said, 'Read such-and-such, for it is the tranquillity (*sakeenah*) that descends when the Qur'an is read, or because of the Qur'an.'"[56]

It is narrated from Abu Sa'eed al-Khudri (رضي الله عنه) that whilst Usayd ibn Ḥudayr was reading Qur'an one night in his *mirbad* (place for drying dates), his horse startled. Then he read some more and his horse startled again. He read some more and his horse startled again. Usayd said: "I was afraid that it would step on Yaḥyaa, so I got up and went to it, and saw something like a shadow above its head, in which there were things like lights. It ascended into the sky until it disappeared."

The following morning I went to the Messenger of Allah (ﷺ) and said, 'O Messenger of Allah, last night whilst I was reading Qur'an at midnight in my *mirbad*, my horse startled.' The Messenger of Allah said, 'Read, O son of Ḥudayr.' He said, 'I read some more, and my horse got startled again.' The Messenger of Allah said, 'Read, O son of Ḥudayr.' He said, 'I read some more, and my horse got startled again.' The Messenger of Allah said, 'Read, O son of Ḥudayr.' He said, 'So I stopped. Yaḥyaa was near it (the horse) and I was afraid that it would step on him, then I saw something like a shadow in which were things like lights. It ascended into the sky until it disappeared.'

The Messenger of Allah (ﷺ) said: 'That was the angels who were listening to you. If you had continued to read, they would have become visible to the people in the morning and they would not have hidden from them.'[57]

---

[56] Muslim, 1/548, hadith no. 796.

[57] Bukhaari, 9/63, hadith no. 5018, from Muhammad ibn Ibraaheem from Usayd ibn Ḥudayr. Also narrated by Muslim, 1/458, hadith no. 796. This version is narrated by Muslim.

(x) They convey the *salaams* of the ummah to the Messenger (ﷺ)

An-Nasaa'i and Ad-Daarimi narrated that 'Abd-Allah ibn Mas'ood said: "The Messenger of Allah (ﷺ) said: 'Allah has angels travelling about the earth to convey to me the *salaams* of my ummah.'"[58]

(xi) They give glad tidings to the believers

They brought glad tidings to the Prophet Ibraaheem that he would be blessed with righteous offspring:

﴿هَلْ أَتَىٰكَ حَدِيثُ ضَيْفِ إِبْرَٰهِيمَ ٱلْمُكْرَمِينَ ﴿٢٤﴾ إِذْ دَخَلُوا۟ عَلَيْهِ فَقَالُوا۟ سَلَـٰمًا ۖ قَالَ سَلَـٰمٌ قَوْمٌ مُّنكَرُونَ ﴿٢٥﴾ فَرَاغَ إِلَىٰٓ أَهْلِهِۦ فَجَآءَ بِعِجْلٍ سَمِينٍ ﴿٢٦﴾ فَقَرَّبَهُۥٓ إِلَيْهِمْ قَالَ أَلَا تَأْكُلُونَ ﴿٢٧﴾ فَأَوْجَسَ مِنْهُمْ خِيفَةً ۖ قَالُوا۟ لَا تَخَفْ ۖ وَبَشَّرُوهُ بِغُلَـٰمٍ عَلِيمٍ ﴿٢٨﴾﴾

﴾Has the story reached you, of the honoured guests [three angels; Jibreel (Gabriel) along with another two] of Ibraaheem [Abraham]? When they came in to him and said: '*Salaam*, [peace be upon you]!' He answered: '*Salaam*, [peace be upon you],' and said: 'You are a people unknown to me.'
Then he turned to his household, and brought out a roasted calf [as the property of Ibraaheem (Abraham) was mainly cows].
And placed it before them [saying]: 'Will you not eat?'
Then he conceived fear of them [when they ate not]. They said: 'Fear not.' And they gave him glad tidings of a son having knowledge [about Allah and His religion of True Monotheism].﴿

(Qur'an 51:24-28)

They brought Prophet Zakariya the glad tidings of Yaḥyaa:

﴿فَنَادَتْهُ ٱلْمَلَـٰٓئِكَةُ وَهُوَ قَآئِمٌ يُصَلِّى فِى ٱلْمِحْرَابِ أَنَّ ٱللَّهَ يُبَشِّرُكَ بِيَحْيَىٰ ﴿٣٩﴾﴾

﴾Then the angels called him, while he was standing in prayer in *Al-Miḥraab* [a praying place or a private room], [saying]: 'Allah gives you glad tidings of Yaḥyaa [John]'.﴿ *(Qur'an 3:39)*

---

[58] *Mishkaat al-Maṣaabeeḥ*, 1/291, no. 924. The editor of *Al-Mishkaat*, Shaykh Naaṣir ad-Deen al-Albaani, said: its *isnaad* is *ṣaḥeeḥ*. It is classed as *ṣaḥeeḥ* by Al-Ḥaakim and Adh-Dhahabi agreed with him.

This is not limited only to the Prophets and Messengers; the angels may also bring glad tidings to the believers. In *Ṣaḥeeḥ Muslim* it is narrated from Abu Hurayrah that the Prophet (ﷺ) said: "A man visited a brother of his in another town, and Allah sent an angel to wait for him on the road. When the man passed by him, the angel said, 'Where are you going?' He said, 'To a brother of mine in this town.' The angel said, 'Is there a favour that you owe him?' The man said, 'No, but I love him for the sake of Allah.' He said, 'I am a messenger from Allah to you, to tell you that Allah loves you as you love him.'"[59]

In *Ṣaḥeeḥ al-Bukhaari* and *Ṣaḥeeḥ Muslim*, it is narrated that Abu Hurayrah said: "The Messenger of Allah (ﷺ) said: 'Jibreel came to me and said, 'O Messenger of Allah, Khadeejah is coming to you with a vessel in which is some food or drink. When she comes to you, convey to her greetings of *salaam* from her Lord and from me, and give her the glad tidings of a house in Paradise made of *qaṣab,*[60] in which there is no noise or exhaustion.''"[61]

(xii) The angels and dreams

Bukhaari narrated in his *Ṣaḥeeḥ* in *Baab at-Tahajjud*, that 'Abd-Allah ibn 'Umar (رضي الله عنه) said: "At the time of the Prophet (ﷺ), if a man saw a dream, he would tell it to the Messenger of Allah (ﷺ). I wished that I would see a dream so that I could tell it to the Messenger of Allah (ﷺ). I was a young lad, and I used to sleep in the mosque at the time of the Messenger of Allah (ﷺ). I saw in a dream that two angels took me and brought me to the Fire, which was built up all around like a built well, and it had two poles in it. There were some people in it whom I recognized, and I started to say, 'I seek refuge with Allah from the Fire.' Then I met another angel who said to me, 'Do not be afraid.'"[62]

---

[59] Muslim, 4/1988, no. 2567.

[60] *Qaṣab*: Pipes made of gold or pearls and other precious stones (The Translation of the Meanings of *Ṣaḥeeḥ al-Bukhaari*, Vol. 3, p. 12) (Translator).

[61] Bukhaari, 7/133, no. 3820. Also narrated by Muslim, 4/1887, no. 232. This version is narrated by Muslim.

[62] Bukhaari, 3/6, no. 1121. Muslim, 4/1927, no. 2479.

In *Ṣaḥeeḥ al-Bukhaari* it is narrated that 'Aa'ishah (may Allah be pleased with her) said: "The Messenger of Allah (ﷺ) said to me, 'I saw you in a dream. An angel brought you to me wrapped up in silk. He said to me, 'This is your wife.' I lifted the cloth from your face and saw that it was you. I said, 'If this dream is from Allah then it will surely come to pass.'"'[63]

(xiii) They fight alongside the believers and support them at times of war

Allah supported the believers with many of the angels at the battle of Badr:

﴿إِذْ تَسْتَغِيثُونَ رَبَّكُمْ فَٱسْتَجَابَ لَكُمْ أَنِّى مُمِدُّكُم بِأَلْفٍ مِّنَ ٱلْمَلَٰٓئِكَةِ
مُرْدِفِينَ ﴿٩﴾﴾

﴾[Remember] when you sought help of your Lord and He answered you [saying]: 'I will help you with a thousand of the angels each behind the other [following one another] in succession.'﴿

(Qur'an 8:9)

﴿وَلَقَدْ نَصَرَكُمُ ٱللَّهُ بِبَدْرٍ وَأَنتُمْ أَذِلَّةٌ ۖ فَٱتَّقُوا۟ ٱللَّهَ لَعَلَّكُمْ تَشْكُرُونَ ﴿١٢٣﴾ إِذْ تَقُولُ
لِلْمُؤْمِنِينَ أَلَن يَكْفِيَكُمْ أَن يُمِدَّكُمْ رَبُّكُم بِثَلَٰثَةِ ءَالَٰفٍ مِّنَ ٱلْمَلَٰٓئِكَةِ مُنزَلِينَ ﴿١٢٤﴾
بَلَىٰٓ ۚ إِن تَصْبِرُوا۟ وَتَتَّقُوا۟ وَيَأْتُوكُم مِّن فَوْرِهِمْ هَٰذَا يُمْدِدْكُمْ رَبُّكُم بِخَمْسَةِ ءَالَٰفٍ مِّنَ
ٱلْمَلَٰٓئِكَةِ مُسَوِّمِينَ ﴿١٢٥﴾﴾

﴾And Allah has already made you victorious at Badr, when you were a weak little force. So fear Allah much that you may be grateful. [Remember] when you [Muhammad] said to the believers, 'Is it not enough for you that your Lord [Allah] should help you with three thousand angels sent down?

Yes, if you hold on to patience and piety, and the enemy comes

---

[63] This version is narrated by Bukhaari in *Kitaab an-Nikaaḥ*, 9/180, no. 5125. Also narrated in *Manaaqib al-Anṣaar*, 7/223, no. 3895; and in *At-Ta'beer*, 12/399, no. 7011, 7012. Also narrated by Muslim, 4/1889, no. 2438.

> rushing at you; your Lord will help you with five thousand angels having marks [of distinction].'》 *(Qur'an 3:123-125)*

In *Ṣaḥeeḥ al-Bukhaari* it is narrated from Ibn 'Abbaas that the Messenger (ﷺ) said on the day of Badr: "This is Jibreel who has taken up his horse's reins and is dressed for battle."[64]

Allah has explained the reason for this angelic support, which is to strengthen the believers, to fight alongside them, and to fight the enemies of Allah and kill them by striking their necks and hands:

﴿وَمَا جَعَلَهُ ٱللَّهُ إِلَّا بُشْرَىٰ وَلِتَطْمَئِنَّ بِهِۦ قُلُوبُكُمْ ۚ وَمَا ٱلنَّصْرُ إِلَّا مِنْ عِندِ ٱللَّهِ ۚ
إِنَّ ٱللَّهَ عَزِيزٌ حَكِيمٌ ﴿١٠﴾﴾

> 《Allah made it only as glad tidings, and that your hearts be at rest therewith. And there is no victory except from Allah. Verily, Allah is All-Mighty, All-Wise.》 *(Qur'an 8:10)*

﴿إِذْ يُوحِى رَبُّكَ إِلَى ٱلْمَلَٰٓئِكَةِ أَنِّى مَعَكُمْ فَثَبِّتُوا۟ ٱلَّذِينَ ءَامَنُوا۟ ۚ سَأُلْقِى فِى قُلُوبِ ٱلَّذِينَ
كَفَرُوا۟ ٱلرُّعْبَ فَٱضْرِبُوا۟ فَوْقَ ٱلْأَعْنَاقِ وَٱضْرِبُوا۟ مِنْهُمْ كُلَّ بَنَانٍ ﴿١٢﴾﴾

> 《[Remember] when your Lord revealed to the angels, 'Verily, I am with you, so keep firm those who have believed. I will cast terror into the hearts of those who have disbelieved, so strike them over the necks, and smite over all their fingers and toes.'》 *(Qur'an 8:12)*

And Allah says in *Soorat Aal 'Imraan*:

﴿وَمَا جَعَلَهُ ٱللَّهُ إِلَّا بُشْرَىٰ لَكُمْ وَلِتَطْمَئِنَّ قُلُوبُكُم بِهِۦ ۗ وَمَا ٱلنَّصْرُ إِلَّا مِنْ عِندِ ٱللَّهِ
ٱلْعَزِيزِ ٱلْحَكِيمِ ﴿١٢٦﴾ لِيَقْطَعَ طَرَفًا مِّنَ ٱلَّذِينَ كَفَرُوٓا۟ أَوْ يَكْبِتَهُمْ فَيَنقَلِبُوا۟ خَآئِبِينَ ﴿١٢٧﴾﴾

> 《Allah made it not but as a message of good news for you and as an assurance to your hearts. And there is no victory except from Allah, the All-Mighty, the All-Wise.
> That He might cut off a part of those who disbelieve, or expose them

---

[64] Bukhaari, 7/312, no. 3995.

to infamy, so that they retire frustrated.﴿ *(Qur'an 3:126-127)*

One of the Muslim fighters heard the sound of a blow struck by an angel, when he struck one of the *kuffaar*, and he heard his voice as he was urging his horse forward. In *Ṣaḥeeḥ Muslim* it is narrated that Ibn 'Abbaas said: "On that day, when one of the Muslim men was pursuing one of the *mushrikeen*, he heard the crack of a whip above his head, and the voice of a horseman saying, 'Go forth, Ḥayzam!' He looked at the *mushrik* in front of him and saw that he had fallen on his back. He looked again and saw that his nose had been cut off and his face was cut, as if it had been struck with a whip, and he had turned green. The *Anṣaari* came and told the Messenger of Allah (ﷺ) about that, and he said, 'You have spoken the truth. That was one of the troops of the third heaven.'"[65]

The angels also fought in other battles. During the campaign of *Al-Khandaq* (the Ditch), Allah sent His angels:

﴿يَٰٓأَيُّهَا ٱلَّذِينَ ءَامَنُوا۟ ٱذْكُرُوا۟ نِعْمَةَ ٱللَّهِ عَلَيْكُمْ إِذْ جَآءَتْكُمْ جُنُودٌ فَأَرْسَلْنَا عَلَيْهِمْ رِيحًا
وَجُنُودًا لَّمْ تَرَوْهَا ﴿٩﴾﴾

﴾O you who believe! Remember Allah's Favour to you, when there came against you hosts, and We sent against them a wind and forces that you saw not [i.e. troops of angels during the battle of *Al Aḥzaab* (the Confederates)].﴿ *(Qur'an 33:9)*

What is meant by the "forces that you saw not" is the angels, as it is reported in the books of *Ṣaḥeeḥ* and elsewhere that Jibreel came to the Messenger (ﷺ) after he had returned from *Al-Khandaq* (the Ditch) and had laid down his arms and bathed. Jibreel came to him, brushing the dust from his head, and said to the Messenger (ﷺ), "Have you laid down your arms? By Allah, we (angels) have not yet laid down our arms. Go out to them." The Messenger of Allah (ﷺ) said, "Where to?" and he pointed towards Banu Qurayẓah.[66]

---

[65] Muslim, 3/1384, hadith no. 1763.

[66] Bukhaari, 7/407, no. 4117. Muslim, 3/1389, hadith no. 1769.

In *Ṣaḥeeḥ al-Bukhaari* it is narrated that Anas (رضي الله عنه) said: "It is as if I can see the dust clearly in the area of Banu Ghanam, and the troops of Jibreel when the Messenger of Allah (ﷺ) set out for Banu Qurayzah."[67]

(xiv) Their protection of the Messenger (ﷺ)

Muslim narrated in his *Saheeh* that Abu Hurayrah (رضي الله عنه) said: "Abu Jahl said, 'Has Muhammad rubbed his face in the dust among you?' They said, 'Yes.' He said, 'By Al-Laat and Al-'Uzza, if I see him doing that, I will step on his neck, or I will rub his face in the dust!'

Then he came to the Messenger of Allah (ﷺ) whilst he was praying, and announced that he was going to step on his neck. Then suddenly he turned on his heels and fled, folding his hands over his face. Someone asked him, 'What's wrong with you?' He said, 'There is a ditch of fire between me and him, and terror, and wings.' The Messenger of Allah (ﷺ) said, 'If he had come any closer to me, the angels would have snatched him away.'"[68]

A shorter version of this is narrated by Bukhaari, in *Kitaab al-Tafseer.*[69]

(xv) They protect and support righteous people, and relieve their distress

Allah may send angels to protect some of His righteous slaves other than the Prophets and Messengers. This may be what happened to a man whose story is told by Ibn Katheer. In *Tafseer Ibn Katheer*, in the commentary on the *aayah* –

﴿أَمَّن يُجِيبُ ٱلْمُضْطَرَّ إِذَا دَعَاهُ ﴿٦٢﴾﴾

﴿Is not He [better than your gods] Who responds to the distressed one, when he calls on Him.﴾ *(Qur'an 27:62)* -

---

[67] Bukhaari, 7/407, hadith no. 4118.

[68] Muslim, 4/2154, hadith no. 2797

[69] Bukhaari, 8/724, hadith no. 4958.

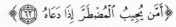

He said:

Al-Ḥaafiẓ ibn 'Asaakir mentioned the story of a man of whom Abu Bakr Muḥammad ibn Dawood ad-Daynoori, who was known as Ad-Daqqi aṣ-Ṣoofi. This man said: "I used to transport people and their goods with a mule that belonged to me, from Damascus to Balad az-Zabadaani. One day a man rode with me, and for part of the way we were travelling off the beaten track. He said to me, 'Take this path, it is shorter.' I said, 'That's no good.' He said, 'But it is shorter.'

So we took that path, and it reached a place where it was very difficult to go, and there was a deep valley in which there were many dead bodies. He said, 'Hold the mule's head, so I can dismount.' He dismounted, then he rolled up his sleeves and gathered up his garments. Then he pulled out a knife and came towards me. I ran away from him, and he followed me. I implored him by Allah, and said, 'Take the mule and all the baggage on it!' He said, 'They are mine anyway, but I am going to kill you!' I tried to scare him by reminding him of Allah and the punishment, but he paid no heed to that.

So I surrendered to him, and I said, 'Let me pray two *rak'ahs*.' He said, 'Hurry up, then!' So I stood up to pray, but the words of the Qur'an would not come to me. I could not remember even a single letter. I remained standing, confused, and he was saying, 'Come on! Get on with it!' Then Allah enabled me to recite,

﴿أَمَّن يُجِيبُ ٱلْمُضْطَرَّ إِذَا دَعَاهُ وَيَكْشِفُ ٱلسُّوٓءَ ﴿٦٢﴾﴾

> ﴿'Is not He [better than your gods] Who responds to the distressed one, when he calls on Him, and Who removes the evil.'﴾
>
> *(Qur'an 27:62)*

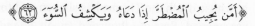

Suddenly I saw a horseman who had come from the mouth of the valley, with a spear in his hand. He threw the spear at the man, and it did not miss his heart. The man fell down dead, and I clung to the horseman and said, 'By Allah, who are you?' He said, 'I am a messenger of the One Who responds to the distressed one when he calls on Him, and Who removes the evil.' Then I took the mule and the baggage, and returned safe and sound."

Similarly, Allah sent Jibreel to help the mother of Ismaa'eel in Makkah. In *Ṣaḥeeḥ al-Bukhaari* it is narrated from Ibn 'Abbaas from the Prophet (ﷺ), in the story of Ibraaheem's migration with Ismaa'eel and his mother Ḥaajir to the land of Makkah – which is a long story – that the mother of Ismaa'eel ran like a distressed person between Aṣ-Ṣafa' and Al-Marwah seven times, looking for water. "When she looked out from Al-Marwah, she heard a voice, and she kept quiet and listened attentively. She heard the voice again and said, "O (whoever you may be)! You have made me hear your voice; have you got something to help me?" And she saw an angel at the place of Zamzam, digging the earth with his heel (or his wing), till water flowed from that place... The angel said to her, 'Don't be afraid of being neglected, for this is the House of Allah which will be built by this boy and his father, and Allah never neglects His people.'"[70]

This angel who came to her was Jibreel. In *Al-Musnad* it is narrated from Ibn 'Abbaas that Ubayy ibn Ka'b said: "When Jibreel dug Zamzam with his heel, the mother of Ismaa'eel started to scoop up the earth around it. The Prophet (ﷺ) said: 'May Allah have mercy on Ismaa'eel's mother! Had she left Zamzam alone (flowing without trying to control it), Zamzam would have been a stream flowing on the surface of the earth.'"[71]

(xvi) The angels attend the funerals of the righteous

The Messenger (ﷺ) said concerning Sa'd ibn Mu'aadh, "This is the one at whose death the Throne has shaken and for whom the gates of heaven are opened. Seventy thousand angels attended his funeral, and he was squeezed (in his grave) once, then he was released." This is narrated by An-Nasaa'i from Ibn 'Umar.[72]

---

[70] Bukhaari, 6/397, hadith no. 3364.

[71] *Musnad Aḥmad*, 5/121.

[72] The hadith about the Throne shaking at the death of Sa'd is narrated by Muslim, 7/122, hadith no. 3802. It is narrated by Muslim from Jaabir, 4/1915, hadith no. 2466. The report about the angels attending his funeral is narrated in *Sunan an-Nasaa'i*. See *Ṣaḥeeḥ Sunan an-Nasaa'i*, 2/441, no. 1942.

(xvii) They shade the *shaheed* (martyr) with their wings

In Bukhaari it is narrated that Jaabir said: "My father was brought to the Prophet (ﷺ), and his body had been mutilated. He was placed before him [the Prophet (ﷺ)], and I went to uncover his face, my people stopped me from doing so. The sound of wailing could be heard, and it was said that it was the daughter of 'Amr, or the sister of 'Amr. The Prophet (ﷺ) said, "Why are you weeping? The angels are still shading him with their wings."

Bukhaari narrated this in a chapter entitled *Baab Ẓill al-Malaa'ikah 'ala'sh-Shaheed* (Chapter: The Angels' Shading of the Martyr).[73]

(xviii) The angels who brought the Ark of the Covenant (*At-Taaboot*)

﴿وَقَالَ لَهُمْ نَبِيُّهُمْ إِنَّ ءَايَةَ مُلْكِهِۦٓ أَن يَأْتِيَكُمُ ٱلتَّابُوتُ فِيهِ
سَكِينَةٌ مِّن رَّبِّكُمْ وَبَقِيَّةٌ مِّمَّا تَرَكَ ءَالُ مُوسَىٰ وَءَالُ هَٰرُونَ تَحْمِلُهُ
ٱلْمَلَٰٓئِكَةُ ۚ (٢٤٨)﴾

﴾And their Prophet [Samuel] said to them: 'Verily! The sign of His kingdom is that there shall come to you *At-Taaboot* [a wooden box], wherein is *Sakeenah* [peace and reassurance] from your Lord and a remnant of that which Moosa [Moses] and Haaroon [Aaron] left behind, carried by the angels.'﴿ *(Qur'an 2:248)*

What we learn from this *aayah* is that the angels brought to the Children of Israel at that time this wooden box (*taaboot*) to reassure them, so that they might know that *Taaloot* (Saul) was chosen by Allah, so they should follow him and obey him.

(xix) They will protect Makkah and Madeenah from the *Dajjaal*

When the *Dajjaal* emerges, he will enter every city except Makkah and Madeenah, because the angels are protecting them. This is reported in *Ṣaḥeeḥ Muslim* from Faaṭimah bint Qays, from the story of Tameem ad-Daari, in which it says that the *Dajjaal* said: "I am *Al-Maseeḥ ad-Dajjaal*

[73] Bukhaari, 6/32, no. 2816.

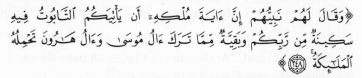

(the "Pseudo Christ"). Soon I will be granted permission to emerge and I will emerge and travel throughout the earth. There will be no town which I will not enter, during a period of forty days, apart from Makkah and Ṭeebah. They are both forbidden for me; every time I try to enter one of them, I will be met by an angel with an unsheathed sword in his hand, who will prevent me from entering it. At every gate there is an angel guarding it."

She (Faaṭimah bint Qays) said: "The Messenger of Allah (ﷺ) said, striking the *minbar* with his stick, "This is Ṭeebah, this is Ṭeebah, this is Ṭeebah," meaning Al-Madeenah.[74]

Bukhaari narrated from Abu Bakrah that the Prophet (ﷺ) said: "The terror of *Al-Maseeḥ ad-Dajjaal* will not enter Madeenah. At that time it will have seven gates, at each of which will be two angels."[75]

In *Ṣaḥeeḥ al-Bukhaari* it is narrated from Abu Hurayrah that the Messenger (ﷺ) said: "At the gates of Madeenah there are angels; neither the plague nor the *Dajjaal* will enter it."[76]

(xx) 'Eesa will descend in the company of the angels

In *Sunan at-Tirmidhi*, it is narrated from An-Nawaas ibn Sam'aan that in the hadith about the *Dajjaal*, the Prophet (ﷺ) said, "Whilst he is like that, 'Eesa ibn Maryam will come down at the white minaret, in the east of Damascus, wearing two garments lightly dyed with saffron, placing his hands on the wings of two angels."[77]

(xxi) The angels spread their wings over Ash-Shaam (Syria)

It is narrated that Zayd ibn Thaabit al-Anṣaari (رضي الله عنه) said: "I heard the Messenger of Allah (ﷺ) say, 'How blessed is Ash-Shaam (Present day

---

[74] Muslim, 4/2264, hadith no. 2942.

[75] Bukhaari, 13/90, hadith no. 7125.

[76] Bukhaari, 13/101, hadith no. 7123.

[77] The descent of 'Eesa (عليه السلام) is proven in Muslim, 4/2259, hadith no. 2940. The hadith mentioned is narrated by At-Tirmidhi. See *Ṣaḥeeḥ Sunan at-Tirmidhi*, 2/249, no. 1825.

Syria, Jordan and Palestine) how blessed is Ash-Shaam!' They said, 'O Messenger of Allah, why is that?' He said, 'The angels of Allah spread their wings over Ash-Shaam.'"[78]

(xxii) The reward in coinciding with the angels

It is narrated in *Ṣaḥeeḥayn* (Bukhaari and Muslim) that the Messenger of Allah (ﷺ) said: "When the Imaam says *Ameen*, say *Ameen*, for whoever's saying *Ameen* coincides with the *Ameen* of the angels, all his previous sins will be forgiven."[79]

In *Ṣaḥeeḥ al-Bukhaari*: "If one of you says *Ameen* and the angels in heaven say *Ameen*, and they coincide with one another, all his previous sins will be forgiven."[80]

In *Ṣaḥeeḥ al-Bukhaari* it is narrated from Abu Hurayrah (رضي الله عنه) that the Prophet (ﷺ) said: "When the Imaam says *'Sami' Allahu liman ḥamidah,'* say, *'Rabbanaa wa laka'l-ḥamd.'* Whoever's words coincide with those of the angels, all his previous sins will be forgiven."[81]

(2) The obligations of the believers towards the angels

The angels are slaves of Allah, whom He has chosen especially, and they have a high status with their Lord. The believer who worships Allah and seeks His pleasure has no alternative but to regard the angels as friends and view them with love and respect, and to avoid anything that may

---

[78] Shaykh Naaṣir said, in *Takhreej Aḥaadeeth Fadaa'il ash-Shaam*, of the hadith narrated by Al-Raba'i: It is a *ṣaḥeeḥ* hadith which is narrated by At-Tirmidhi, by Al-Ḥaakim in *Al-Mustadrak*, and by Aḥmad in *Al-Musnad*. Al-Ḥaakim said, it is *ṣaḥeeḥ* according to the conditions of the two *shaykhs* Bukhaari and Muslim, and Adh-Dhahabi agreed with him. And it is as they said. Al-Mundhiri said in *At-Targheeb wat-Tarheeb*, it is narrated by Ibn Ḥibbaan in his *Ṣaḥeeḥ*, and by Aṭ-Ṭabaraani with a *ṣaḥeeḥ isnaad*.

[79] Bukhaari, 2/262, hadith no. 780. Also narrated by Muslim, 1/307, hadith no. 410.

[80] Bukhaari, 2/266, hadith no. 781.

[81] Bukhaari, 2/283, hadith no. 796.

result in annoying or offending them. We will discuss this matter in further detail below:

(i) Not offending the angels

The scholars emphatically denounced those who slander the angels or speak badly of them. Al-'Allaamah as-Suyooṭi (may Allah have mercy on him) said: "Al-Qaḍi 'Iyaaḍ said in *Ash-Shifaa'*: Sahnoon said: whoever insults one of the angels should be executed. Abu'l-Ḥasan al-Qaabisi said concerning a person who says of another, 'He looks like the angry Maalik (keeper of Hell),' if it is known that his intention was to slander the angel, he should be executed.

Al-Qaḍi 'Iyaaḍ said: This is concerning one who insults them all in general, or who insults by name one of those who is proven to be an angel, because Allah has mentioned him in the Qur'an or we know from the *mutawaatir aḥaadeeth* that he is an angel, or it is known by definitive scholarly consensus that he is an angel, such as Jibreel, Mikaa'eel, Maalik, the keepers of Paradise and Hell, the angels of Hell, the bearers of the Throne, 'Azraa'eel, Israafeel, Riḍwaan, the guardian angels, and Munkar and Nakeer.

But with regard to those who are not proven to be angels, and concerning whom there is no scholarly consensus that they are angels, such as Haaroot and Maaroot, this ruling does not apply. The one who disbelieves in them is not subject to the same ruling as mentioned above, because there is no definitive report to show that they have the same status as the angels."[82]

Suyooṭi quoted Al-Qaraafi al-Maaliki as saying: "Know that it is obligatory upon every accountable person to respect all of the Prophets and all of the angels. Whoever slanders their honour in any way is a *kaafir*, whether he does so implicitly or explicitly. Whoever says of a man who he thinks is very harsh, 'He is more harsh than Maalik, the keeper of Hell,' or of a man who is deformed, 'He is uglier than Munkar

---

[82] *Al-Ḥabaa'ik fi Akhbaar al-Malaa'ik*, by Suyooṭi, 254.

and Nakeer', is a *kaafir*, if he says that in the context of condemning ugliness and harshness."[83]

(ii) Keeping away from sin and disobedience

The things which most offend the angels are sin, disobedience to Allah, *kufr* and *shirk*. Hence the best gift that a man can give to the angels and the thing which is most pleasing to them is for a man to be sincerely devoted in his religious commitment to his Lord, and to avoid everything that angers Him.

Hence the angels do not enter places and houses where Allah is disobeyed, or in which there are things which Allah dislikes and hates, such as stone altars, statues and pictures. And they do not come near people who indulge in sin, such as drunkards.

Ibn Katheer[84] said: It is reported in the *aḥaadeeth* narrated in the books of *Ṣaḥeeḥ*, *Musnad* and *Sunan* from a group of the *Ṣaḥaabah* that the Messenger of Allah (ﷺ) said: "The angels do not enter a house in which there is an image, a dog or a person who is *junub* (in a state of ritual impurity)."

According to a report narrated from 'Aasim ibn Damurah from 'Ali, "... and not urine." According to a *marfoo'* report narrated from Abu Sa'eed: "The angels do not enter a house in which there is a dog or a statue." According to the report of Dhakwaan Abu Ṣaliḥ al-Sammaak from Abu Hurayrah, he said: "The Messenger of Allah (ﷺ) said: 'The angels do not accompany a group with whom there is a dog or a bell.'"[85]

Al-Bazzaar narrated with a *ṣaḥeeḥ isnaad* from Buraydah (رضي الله عنه) that the Messenger (ﷺ) said: "There are three whom the angels do not come near: the one who is drunk, the one who is perfumed with saffron and the one who is *junub* (in a state of ritual impurity)."[86]

---

[83] *Al-Habaa'ik fi Akhbaar al-Malaa'ik*, by Suyooṭi, 255.

[84] *Al-Bidaayah wan-Nihaayah*, 1/55.

[85] *Al-Bidaayah wan-Nihaayah*, 1/55.

[86] *Ṣaḥeeḥ al-Jaami'*, 3/70.

In *Sunan Abi Dawood* it is narrated with a *ḥasan isnaad* from 'Ammaar ibn Yaasir that the Messenger (ﷺ) said: "There are three things which the angels do not come near: the dead body of a *kaafir*, the one who is perfumed with saffron and the person who is *junub* (in a state of ritual impurity), unless he performs *wuḍoo'*."[87]

(iii) The angels are offended by that which offends the sons of Adam

It is reported in the *ṣaḥeeḥ aḥaadeeth* that the angels are offended by that which offends the sons of Adam. So they are offended by offensive smells and by filth and dirt.

Bukhaari and Muslim narrated from Jaabir ibn 'Abd-Allah that the Prophet (ﷺ) said: "Whoever eats garlic, onions or leeks, let him not come near our mosque, for the angels are offended by that which offends the sons of Adam."[88]

The matter is so serious that the Messenger (ﷺ) ordered the one who came to the mosque emanating the smell of garlic or onions to go out to *Al-Baqee'*.[89]

(iv) The prohibition on spitting to the right whilst praying

The Messenger (ﷺ) forbade spitting to the right during prayer, because when a person stands up to pray, an angel stands on his right. In *Ṣaḥeeḥ al-Bukhaari* it is narrated from Abu Hurayrah that the Prophet (ﷺ) said: "When anyone of you stands up to pray, let him not spit to the front, for he is conversing with Allah so long as he is praying. And there is an angel standing to his right, so let him spit to his left or beneath his foot, then bury it."[90]

---

[87] *Ṣaḥeeḥ Sunan Abi Dawood*, 2/872.

[88] The *aḥaadeeth* which forbid those who have eaten onions and garlic from coming near the mosque are narrated in *Ṣaḥeeḥ al-Bukhaari*, *Ṣaḥeeḥ Muslim* and elsewhere, but this version is narrated by Muslim, 1/394, hadith no. 567.

[89] Muslim, 1/396, hadith no. 567.

[90] Bukhaari, 1/512, hadith no. 416.

(v) Befriending all the angels

The Muslim has to like all the angels without any discrimination between one angel and another in that regard, because they are all the slaves of Allah who do that which He commands and abstain from that which He prohibits. In this sense they are all the same, and they do not differ at all. The Jews claimed that they had friends and enemies among the angels; they claimed that Jibreel was an enemy to them and that Mikaa'eel was a friend to them. But Allah showed them to be liars in what they were claiming, and stated that there is no difference among the angels.

﴿قُلْ مَن كَانَ عَدُوًّا لِّجِبْرِيلَ فَإِنَّهُۥ نَزَّلَهُۥ عَلَىٰ قَلْبِكَ بِإِذْنِ ٱللَّهِ مُصَدِّقًا لِّمَا
بَيْنَ يَدَيْهِ وَهُدًى وَبُشْرَىٰ لِلْمُؤْمِنِينَ ﴿٩٧﴾ مَن كَانَ عَدُوًّا لِّلَّهِ وَمَلَٰٓئِكَتِهِۦ
وَرُسُلِهِۦ وَجِبْرِيلَ وَمِيكَىٰلَ فَإِنَّ ٱللَّهَ عَدُوٌّ لِّلْكَٰفِرِينَ ﴿٩٨﴾﴾

> ﴿Say [O Muhammad]: 'Whoever is an enemy to Jibreel [Gabriel] [let him die in his fury], for indeed he has brought it [this Qur'an] down to your heart by Allah's Permission, confirming what came before it [i.e. the *Tawraat* (Torah) and the *Injeel* (Gospel)] and guidance and glad tidings for the believers.
>
> Whoever is an enemy to Allah, His Angels, His Messengers, Jibreel [Gabriel] and Mikaa'eel [Michael], then verily, Allah is an enemy to the disbelievers.'﴾ *(Qur'an 2:97-98)*

Allah has told us that the angels are all the same, and whoever takes one of them as an enemy has taken Allah and all the angels as enemies. Liking some of the angels and hating others is a myth which no one could accept apart from the followers of deviant *kufr* like the Jews. This Jewish opinion which is described in the Qur'an is a poor excuse which they gave for not believing. They claimed that Jibreel was their enemy because he comes with war and destruction, and if the one who had come to the Messenger (ﷺ) had been Mikaa'eel, they would have followed him.

See the texts narrated about the reasons for the revelation of this *aayah* in *Tafseer Ibn Katheer* and elsewhere.

4 - THE ANGELS AND THE *KUFFAAR* AND EVILDOERS

In the previous section, we discussed the relationship between angels and the believers. From this it is clear what their relationship with the *kuffaar* is like. They do not like the *kuffaar*, wrongdoers and criminals; rather, they take them as enemies and wage war against them, and create fear in their hearts, as happened at the battles of Badr and *Al-Aḥzaab* (Confederates). This will be discussed in more detail below.

(1) Bringing the punishment down upon the *kuffaar*

When one of the Messengers was rejected and disbelieved, and his people persisted in their rejection, Allah would often send down His punishment upon them. Sometimes those who carried out the punishment were the angels.

(2) Their destruction of the people of the Prophet Looṭ

The angels who were commanded to punish the people of the Prophet Looṭ came in the form of young men with handsome faces. Prophet Looṭ offered them hospitality, and his people did not know about them, but Looṭ's wife told her people about them and they came quickly, wanting to commit evil actions with them. The Prophet Looṭ tried to ward them off and argue with them, but they ignored him. Then Jibreel struck them with his wing, and blinded their eyes, taking away their sight:

﴿وَلَمَّا جَآءَتْ رُسُلُنَا لُوطًا سِيٓءَ بِهِمْ وَضَاقَ بِهِمْ ذَرْعًا وَقَالَ هَٰذَا يَوْمٌ عَصِيبٌ ﴿٧٧﴾
وَجَآءَهُۥ قَوْمُهُۥ يُهْرَعُونَ إِلَيْهِ وَمِن قَبْلُ كَانُوا۟ يَعْمَلُونَ ٱلسَّيِّـَٔاتِ ۚ قَالَ يَٰقَوْمِ هَٰٓؤُلَآءِ بَنَاتِى
هُنَّ أَطْهَرُ لَكُمْ ۖ فَٱتَّقُوا۟ ٱللَّهَ وَلَا تُخْزُونِ فِى ضَيْفِىٓ ۖ أَلَيْسَ مِنكُمْ رَجُلٌ رَّشِيدٌ ﴿٧٨﴾ قَالُوا۟
لَقَدْ عَلِمْتَ مَا لَنَا فِى بَنَاتِكَ مِنْ حَقٍّ وَإِنَّكَ لَتَعْلَمُ مَا نُرِيدُ ﴿٧٩﴾ قَالَ لَوْ أَنَّ لِى بِكُمْ قُوَّةً أَوْ
ءَاوِىٓ إِلَىٰ رُكْنٍ شَدِيدٍ ﴿٨٠﴾ قَالُوا۟ يَٰلُوطُ إِنَّا رُسُلُ رَبِّكَ لَن يَصِلُوٓا۟ إِلَيْكَ ﴿٨١﴾﴾

﴾And when Our messengers came to Looṭ [Lot], he was grieved on account of them and felt himself straitened for them [lest the town people should approach them to commit sodomy with them]. He said: 'This is a distressful day.'

And his people came rushing towards him, and since aforetime they used to commit crimes [sodomy], he said: 'O my people! Here are my daughters [i.e. the women of the nation], they are purer for you [if you marry them lawfully]. So fear Allah and disgrace me not with regard to my guests! Is there not among you a single rightminded man?'
They said: 'Surely, you know that we have neither any desire nor need of your daughters, and indeed you know well what we want!'
He said: 'Would that I had strength [men] to overpower you, or that I could betake myself to some powerful support [to resist you].'
They [messengers] said: 'O Looṭ [Lot]! Verily, we are the messengers from your Lord! They shall not reach you!'》
(Qur'an 11:77-81)

Ibn Katheer[91] said: they mentioned that Jibreel (عليه السلام) went out against them and struck their faces with the edge of his wing. He destroyed their eyes completely so that there was nothing left, not even a trace... Allah says:

﴿وَلَقَدْ رَٰوَدُوهُ عَن ضَيْفِهِۦ فَطَمَسْنَآ أَعْيُنَهُمْ فَذُوقُوا۟ عَذَابِى وَنُذُرِ ﴿٣٧﴾﴾

﴿And they indeed sought to shame his guest [by asking to commit sodomy with them]. So We blinded their eyes [saying], 'Then taste you My Torment and My Warnings.'》 *(Qur'an 54:37)*

The next morning, Allah destroyed them:

﴿فَلَمَّا جَآءَ أَمْرُنَا جَعَلْنَا عَـٰلِيَهَا سَافِلَهَا وَأَمْطَرْنَا عَلَيْهَا حِجَارَةً مِّن سِجِّيلٍ مَّنضُودٍ ﴿٨٢﴾ مُّسَوَّمَةً عِندَ رَبِّكَ ۖ وَمَا هِىَ مِنَ ٱلظَّـٰلِمِينَ بِبَعِيدٍ ﴿٨٣﴾﴾

﴿So when Our Commandment came, We turned [the towns of Sodom in Palestine] upside down, and rained on them stones of baked clay, in a well-arranged manner one after another;
Marked from your Lord; and they are not ever far from the *Ẓaalimoon* [polytheists, evildoers].》 *(Qur'an 11:82-83)*

---

91 *Al-Bidaayah wan-Nihaayah*, 1/197.

Ibn Katheer said in his *Tafseer*: "Mujaahid said: 'Jibreel seized the people of the Prophet Looṭ from their fields and houses, and carried them with their flocks and possessions. He lifted them up until the inhabitants of heaven heard the barking of their dogs, then he turned them upside down. He carried them on the coverts of his right wing.' He mentioned other similar thing, but he did not narrate any hadith to support that."

(3) Their cursing of the *kuffaar*

Allah, the Almighty, says:

﴿كَيْفَ يَهْدِى ٱللَّهُ قَوْمًا كَفَرُوا۟ بَعْدَ إِيمَـٰنِهِمْ وَشَهِدُوٓا۟ أَنَّ ٱلرَّسُولَ حَقٌّ وَجَآءَهُمُ ٱلْبَيِّنَـٰتُ ۚ وَٱللَّهُ لَا يَهْدِى ٱلْقَوْمَ ٱلظَّـٰلِمِينَ ﴿٨٦﴾ أُو۟لَـٰٓئِكَ جَزَآؤُهُمْ أَنَّ عَلَيْهِمْ لَعْنَةَ ٱللَّهِ وَٱلْمَلَـٰٓئِكَةِ وَٱلنَّاسِ أَجْمَعِينَ ﴿٨٧﴾﴾

﴾How shall Allah guide a people who disbelieved after their Belief and after they bore witness that the Messenger [Muhammad] is true and after clear proofs had come unto them? And Allah guides not the people who are *Ẓaalimoon* [polytheists and wrongdoers].
They are those whose recompense is that on them [rests] the Curse of Allah, of the angels, and of all mankind.﴿ *(Qur'an 3:86-87)*

﴿إِنَّ ٱلَّذِينَ كَفَرُوا۟ وَمَاتُوا۟ وَهُمْ كُفَّارٌ أُو۟لَـٰٓئِكَ عَلَيْهِمْ لَعْنَةُ ٱللَّهِ وَٱلْمَلَـٰٓئِكَةِ وَٱلنَّاسِ أَجْمَعِينَ ﴿١٦١﴾﴾

﴾Verily, those who disbelieve, and die while they are disbelievers, it is they on whom is the Curse of Allah and of the angels and of mankind, combined.﴿ *(Qur'an 2:161)*

The angels do not only curse the *kuffaar*. They may also curse those who commit particular sins, including the following:

(a) The angels curse a woman when she does not respond to her husband

In *Ṣaḥeeḥ al-Bukhaari* it is narrated on the authority of Abu Hurayrah that: "The Messenger of Allah (ﷺ) said: 'When a man calls his wife to his bed and she refuses to come, the angels curse her until morning comes.'"[92] According to another report, "...until she changes her mind."[93]

(b) They curse the one who points towards his brother with a weapon

Muslim narrated in his *Saheeh* that Abu Hurayrah (ﷺ) reported: "Abu'l-Qaasim said: 'Whoever points towards his brother with a weapon is cursed by the angels, even if it is his brother through his father and his mother.'"[94]

The curse of the angels indicates that this action is *haraam*, because it involves frightening one's brother, and because the *Shaytaan* could tempt one to kill one's brother, especially if the weapon is of the modern type which could go off for the slightest mistake or unintentional touch. How often has such a thing happened.

(c) They curse those who slander the Companions of the Messenger

In *Mu'jam at-Tabaraani al-Kabeer* it is narrated from Ibn 'Abbaas with a *hasan isnaad* that the Messenger (ﷺ) said: "Whoever slanders my companions, may there be upon him the curse of Allah, the angels and all of mankind."

How strange it is that some people make slandering the Companions of the Messenger (ﷺ) a religious ritual by means of which they seek to draw closer to Allah, although their punishment is what the Messenger (ﷺ) mentioned in this hadith, and it is a frightening punishment.

(d) They curse those who prevent the shari'ah of Allah from being implemented

In *Sunan an-Nasaa'i* and *Sunan Ibn Maajah* it is narrated with a *saheeh isnaad* from Ibn 'Abbaas (ﷺ) that the Messenger of Allah (ﷺ) said: "Whoever kills (a person) deliberately should be killed in return,

---

[92] Bukhaari, 9/293, hadith no. 5193.

[93] *Ibid*., 9/294, hadith no. 5194.

[94] Muslim, 4/2020, hadith no. 2616.

and whoever tries to prevent that, may he be cursed by Allah, the angels and all of mankind."[95] The one who tries, by means of his wealth or position, to prevent the ruling of Allah from being carried out on one who has deliberately killed another, will be subject to this curse, so how about those who try to prevent the shari'ah from being implemented altogether?

(e) They curse those who give sanctuary to innovators or criminals

Among those who are cursed by the angels and by Allah are those who innovate heresies in Allah's religion and violate His laws, or protect those who do so. It says in a *ṣaḥeeḥ* hadith: "Whoever innovates a heresy or gives sanctuary to an innovator or criminal, may there be upon him the curse of Allah, the angels and all of mankind."[96]

Innovation and criminal actions in Madeenah are even more serious. In *Ṣaḥeeḥayn* (Bukhaari and Muslim) it is narrated that 'Ali ibn Abi Ṭaalib said: "The Prophet (ﷺ) said: 'Madeenah is a sanctuary, from 'Ayr to Thawr (two mountains in Madeenah). Whoever innovates a heresy or commits a crime in (Madeenah), or gives shelter to such a person, may there be upon him the curse of Allah and the angels, and all of mankind, and none of his compulsory or optional good deeds will be accepted on the Day of Resurrection.'"[97]

(4) The demand of the *kuffaar* to see the angels

The *kuffaar* - disbelievers - demanded to see the angels as proof that what the Messenger (ﷺ) said was true. But Allah told them that the Day on which they would see the angels would be a bad day for them. For the *kuffaar* will see the angels when the punishment is about to befall them,

---

[95] *Ṣaḥeeḥ Sunan an-Nasaa'i*, 3/492, no. 4456, 4457. *Ṣaḥeeḥ Sunan Ibn Maajah*, 2/96, no. 2131.

[96] *Ṣaḥeeḥ Sunan Abi Dawood*, 3/859, no. 3797. *Ṣaḥeeḥ Sunan an-Nasaa'i*, 3/982, no. 4412.

[97] Bukhaari, 4/81, hadith no. 1870. Also narrated by Muslim, 2/994, hadith no. 1370. This version is narrated by Muslim.

or when death approaches and the veil is lifted:

﴿وَقَالَ ٱلَّذِينَ لَا يَرْجُونَ لِقَآءَنَا لَوْلَآ أُنزِلَ عَلَيْنَا ٱلْمَلَـٰٓئِكَةُ أَوْ نَرَىٰ رَبَّنَا ۗ لَقَدِ
ٱسْتَكْبَرُوا۟ فِىٓ أَنفُسِهِمْ وَعَتَوْ عُتُوًّا كَبِيرًا ﴿٢١﴾ يَوْمَ يَرَوْنَ ٱلْمَلَـٰٓئِكَةَ لَا بُشْرَىٰ
يَوْمَئِذٍ لِّلْمُجْرِمِينَ وَيَقُولُونَ حِجْرًا مَّحْجُورًا ﴿٢٢﴾﴾

﴾And those who expect not a Meeting with Us [i.e. those who deny the Day of Resurrection and the life of the Hereafter] said: 'Why are not the angels sent down to us, or why do we not see our Lord?' Indeed they think too highly of themselves, and are scornful with great pride.

On the Day they will see the angels no glad tidings will there be for the *Mujrimoon* [criminals, disbelievers, polytheists, sinners] that day. And they [angels] will say: 'All kinds of glad tidings are forbidden to you.'﴿ *(Qur'an 25:21-22)*

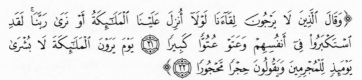

CHAPTER FOUR
THE ANGELS AND OTHER CREATED THINGS

In the previous chapter we discussed the relationship between the angels and the sons of Adam. This is not the only matter with which the angels have been entrusted. The angels also take care of other matters of the universe, things which we can see and things which we cannot see.

We shall limit ourselves to mentioning some of that which has been narrated in the texts.

1 - THE BEARERS OF THE THRONE

The Throne is the greatest of all created things. It encompasses the heavens and is above them, and the Most Merciful is above the Throne, which is borne by eight angels:

﴿وَيَحْمِلُ عَرْشَ رَبِّكَ فَوْقَهُمْ يَوْمَئِذٍ ثَمَٰنِيَةٌ ﴿١٧﴾﴾

﴿And eight angels will, that Day, bear the Throne of your Lord above them.﴾ *(Qur'an 69:17)*[1]

2 - THE ANGELS OF THE MOUNTAIN

There are also angels appointed over the mountains. Allah sent the angel of the mountains to His slave and Messenger Muhammad (ﷺ) to ask his permission to destroy the people of Makkah. In *Ṣaḥeeḥ al-Bukhaari* and *Ṣaḥeeḥ Muslim* it is narrated that 'Aa'ishah said to the Prophet (ﷺ): "O Messenger of Allah, did you ever experience any day that was harder than the day of Uḥud?" He said, "I suffered a great deal from your people, and the worst I suffered from them was the day of 'Aqabah[2],

---

[1] We have already discussed their immense size in the chapter where we discussed their attributes and abilities.

[2] A place in Mina (Author).

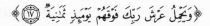

when I called Ibn 'Abd-Yaalayl ibn 'Abd-Kallaal to Islam, and he did not agree to what I was proposing.

So I went away in distress and I did not realize where I was going until I reached Qarn ath-Tha'aalib. Then I raised my head and saw a cloud which was shading me. I looked and I saw Jibreel in it, calling to me. He said, 'Allah has heard what your people have said to you, and how they have responded to you. He has sent the angel of the mountains to you, so that you can command him to do whatever you want to them.'

Then the angel of the mountains called me. He greeted me with *salaams*, then he said: 'O Muhammad, Allah has heard what your people have said to you. I am the angel of the mountains. Your Lord has sent me to you so that you may give me orders. What do you want? If you want I will crush them between Al-Akhshabayn.'[3] The Prophet (ﷺ) said: 'Rather I hope that Allah will bring forth from their loins people who will worship Allah alone, not associating any partner with Him.'"[4]

3 - THE ANGELS WHO ARE APPOINTED OVER RAIN, VEGETATION AND PROVISION

Ibn Katheer[5] said: "Mikaa'eel is appointed over the rain and vegetation from which is created the provision of this world. He has helpers who do whatever he commands them to do by the command of his Lord. They control the winds and clouds as the Lord wills."

Among the angels are those who are responsible for the clouds. In *Sunan at-Tirmidhi* it is narrated from Ibn 'Abbaas that the Messenger of Allah (ﷺ) said: "Ar-Ra'd is one of the angels who is responsible for the clouds... He drives the clouds wherever Allah wills."[6] So rain

---

[3] Two mountains in Makkah (Author).

[4] Muslim, 3/1420, hadith no. 1795. This version is narrated by him. Also narrated by Bukhaari, 6/312, hadith no. 3231.

[5] *Al-Bidaayah wan-Nihaayah*, 1/50.

[6] *Ṣaḥeeḥ Sunan at-Tirmidhi*, 3/64, no. 2492.

may come to one land and not to another, or to one city and not to another.

He may be commanded to send rain on one man's crops, and no one else's, as mentioned in the hadith narrated by Muslim in his *Ṣaḥeeḥ* from Abu Hurayrah, according to which the Prophet (ﷺ) said: "Whilst a man was in the open country, he heard a voice in a cloud (saying), 'Send rain on the garden of so and so.' So the cloud moved and poured down its water in a stony area, and one of the channels took all that water.

He followed the water and found a man standing in his garden, using a shovel to direct the water where he wanted it. He said to him, 'O slave of Allah, what is your name?' He said, 'so and so,' mentioning the name that (the first man) had heard in the cloud. He said, 'O slave of Allah, why did you ask me my name?' He said, 'I heard a voice in the cloud from which this water came, saying, "Send rain on the garden of so and so" and it was your name. What do you do with it?' He said, 'Because you said this, I will tell you. I look at the produce of my garden, then I give one-third in charity, feed myself and my family with one-third, and I put one third back into the garden.'"[7]

Whatever the case, the angels are appointed over the heavens and on earth. Every movement in the universe stems from the angels, as Allah says:

﴿ فَٱلْمُدَبِّرَٰتِ أَمْرًا ﴿٥﴾ ﴾

﴿And by those angels who arrange to do the Commands of their Lord.﴾ *(Qur'an 79:5)*

﴿ فَٱلْمُقَسِّمَٰتِ أَمْرًا ﴿٤﴾ ﴾

﴿And those [angels] who distribute [provisions, rain, and other blessings] by [Allah's] Command.﴾ *(Qur'an 51:4)*

---

[7] Muslim, 4/2288, hadith no. 2984.

Those who reject the Messengers and disbelieve in the Creator claim that it is the stars which do all that, but the ones who do that are the angels, by the command of Allah, as He says:

﴿وَٱلْمُرْسَلَٰتِ عُرْفًا ﴿١﴾ فَٱلْعَٰصِفَٰتِ عَصْفًا ﴿٢﴾ وَٱلنَّٰشِرَٰتِ نَشْرًا ﴿٣﴾ فَٱلْفَٰرِقَٰتِ فَرْقًا ﴿٤﴾ فَٱلْمُلْقِيَٰتِ ذِكْرًا ﴿٥﴾﴾

﴾By the winds [or angels or the Messengers of Allah] sent forth one after another.
And by the winds that blow violently.
And by the winds that scatter clouds and rain.
And by the Verses [of the Qur'an] that separate the right from the wrong.
And by the angels that bring the Revelations to the Messengers.﴿
(Qur'an 77:1-5)

﴿وَٱلنَّٰزِعَٰتِ غَرْقًا ﴿١﴾ وَٱلنَّٰشِطَٰتِ نَشْطًا ﴿٢﴾ وَٱلسَّٰبِحَٰتِ سَبْحًا ﴿٣﴾ فَٱلسَّٰبِقَٰتِ سَبْقًا ﴿٤﴾ فَٱلْمُدَبِّرَٰتِ أَمْرًا ﴿٥﴾﴾

﴾By those [angels] who pull out [the souls of the disbelievers and the wicked] with great violence.
By those [angels] who gently take out [the souls of the believers].
And by those that swim along [i.e. angels or planets in their orbits].
And by those that press forward as in a race [i.e. the angels or stars or the horses].
And by those angels who arrange to do the Commands of their Lord, [so verily, you disbelievers will be called to account].﴿
(Qur'an 79:1-5)

﴿وَٱلصَّٰٓفَّٰتِ صَفًّا ﴿١﴾ فَٱلزَّٰجِرَٰتِ زَجْرًا ﴿٢﴾ فَٱلتَّٰلِيَٰتِ ذِكْرًا ﴿٣﴾﴾

﴾By those [angels] ranged in ranks [or rows].
By those [angels] who drive the clouds in a good way.
By those [angels] who bring the Book and the Qur'an from Allah to mankind.﴿ *(Qur'an 37:1-3)*

All of these *aayaat* speak of the angels when they direct the affairs of the heavens and the earth.

CHAPTER FIVE
WHO IS SUPERIOR - THE ANGELS OR THE SONS OF ADAM?

THIS IS AN ANCIENT DISPUTE

Ibn Katheer[1] said: "The people differed as to whether the angels are superior to mankind. This dispute is mostly to be found in the books of the scholars of *kalaam* (scholastiasm), and the dispute is with the *Mu'tazilah* and those who agreed with them."

The oldest discussion of this matter that I have come across is what is mentioned by Al-Ḥaafiẓ ibn 'Asaakir in his *Taareekh*, where he gives a biography of Umayyah ibn 'Amr ibn Sa'eed ibn al-'Aaṣ: "He attended a gathering with 'Umar ibn 'Abd al-'Azeez, with whom there was a group. 'Umar said: 'There is no one who is dearer to Allah than the good people among the sons of Adam,' and he quoted as evidence the *aayah*,

﴿إِنَّ ٱلَّذِينَ ءَامَنُوا۟ وَعَمِلُوا۟ ٱلصَّٰلِحَٰتِ أُو۟لَٰٓئِكَ هُمْ خَيْرُ ٱلْبَرِيَّةِ ۝٧﴾

> ﴿'Verily, those who believe [in the Oneness of Allah, and in His Messenger (Muhammad) including all obligations ordered by Islam] and do righteous good deeds, they are the best of creatures.'﴾
>
> *(Qur'an 98:7)*

Umayyah ibn 'Amr ibn Sa'eed agreed with him, but 'Arraak ibn Maalik said: 'There is no one dearer to Allah than His angels, who are His servants in this world and in the Hereafter, and His messengers to His Prophets.' And he quoted as evidence the *aayah*:

﴿مَا نَهَىٰكُمَا رَبُّكُمَا عَنْ هَٰذِهِ ٱلشَّجَرَةِ إِلَّآ أَن تَكُونَا مَلَكَيْنِ أَوْ تَكُونَا مِنَ ٱلْخَٰلِدِينَ ۝٢٠﴾

> ﴿He [*Shayṭaan*] said: 'Your Lord did not forbid you this tree save you should become angels or become of the immortals.'﴾
>
> *(Qur'an 7:20)*

---

[1] *Al-Bidaayah wan-Nihaayah*, 1/58.

'Umar ibn 'Abd al-'Azeez said to Muhammad ibn Ka'b al-Quraẓi: 'What do you say, O Abu Ḥamzah?' He said, 'Allah honoured Adam by creating him with His own hand and breathing into him the soul, making the angels prostrate to him, bringing forth from his offspring Prophets, Messengers and those whom the angels visit.'

'Umar ibn 'Abd al-'Azeez agreed with this ruling, and quoted different evidence."

What Ibn Katheer mentioned here about the discussion of 'Umar ibn 'Abd al-'Azeez and his companions on this topic shows that Taaj ad-Deen al-Fazaari was mistaken when he said: "This matter is one of the *bid'ahs* of *'Ilm al-kalaam*, which was not discussed by the early generations of the ummah or by the most knowledgeable of the Imaams after them."[2] Indeed, it is reported that some of the *Ṣaḥaabah* discussed this matter. 'Abd-Allah ibn Salaam said: "Allah never created any creation dearer to Him than Muhammad." It was said to him, "Not even Jibreel and Mikaa'eel?" He said, "Don't you know what Jibreel and Mikaa'eel are? They are two creatures without free will, like the sun and moon. Allah has not created any being dearer to Him than Muhammad (ﷺ)." This is narrated by Al-Ḥaakim in his *Mustadrak* and is rated as *ṣaḥeeḥ* by him and Adh-Dhahabi.[3]

Different views on this matter

The commentator on *Aṭ-Ṭaḥḥaawiyyah* said that the view attributed to *Ahl as-Sunnah* is that only the righteous sons of Adam and the Prophets are superior to the angels. The *Mu'tazilah* say that the angels are better. The followers of Al-Ash'ari are of two views; some of them say that the Prophets and *awliyaa'* are superior, and some refrain from commenting and do not say anything decisive on the matter. It is reported that some of them tended to regard the angels as superior, and this view is also narrated from some of *Ahl as-Sunnah* and some of the Ṣufis.

---

[2] *Sharḥ al-'Aqeedah aṭ-Ṭaḥḥaawiyyah*, 339.

[3] See Al-Albaani's commentary on *Sharḥ al-'Aqeedah aṭ-Ṭaḥḥaawiyyah*, Pp. 342.

The *Shi'ah* said that all of the Imaams are superior to all of the angels. There are other views on this issue also.

No one whose view carries any weight said that the angels are superior to some of the Prophets and not others. It is said that Abu Ḥaneefah (may Allah have mercy on him) declined to answer a question on this matter. The commentator on *At-Ṭaḥhaawiyyah* (may Allah have mercy on him) was also inclined to refrain from making any statement.[4]

As-Safaareeni said that Imaam Aḥmad (may Allah have mercy on him) used to say, "He is mistaken who says that the angels are better." He said, "Every believer is superior to the angels."

The point of dispute

There is no dispute that the *kuffaar* and hypocrites are not included in this discussion of superiority. They are more astray than the animals:

﴿أُولَٰئِكَ كَالْأَنْعَامِ بَلْ هُمْ أَضَلُّ ﴿١٧٩﴾﴾

﴾They are like cattle, nay even more astray.﴿ *(Qur'an 7:179)*

Discussing who is superior does not mean that we are discussing whether the essence of man or the essence of the angels is better. We are discussing whether righteous human beings or angels are superior. Some people say that the angels are better than the believers, so in their case the discussion is whether the Prophets or the angels are superior.

The evidence of those who say that righteous human beings are superior to the angels

Having described the point of the discussion, we will quote the evidence given by those who say that man is superior.

1 - Allah commanded the angels to prostrate to Adam. If he had not been superior, He would not have commanded them to prostrate to him:

---

[4] *Sharḥ al-'Aqeedah aṭ-Ṭaḥḥaawiyyah*, 338.

﴿وَإِذْ قُلْنَا لِلْمَلَٰٓئِكَةِ ٱسْجُدُوا۟ لِءَادَمَ فَسَجَدُوٓا۟ إِلَّآ إِبْلِيسَ أَبَىٰ وَٱسْتَكْبَرَ ﴿٣٤﴾﴾

﴾And [remember] when We said to the angels: 'Prostrate yourselves before Adam.' And they prostrated except *Iblees* [Satan], he refused and was proud.﴿ *(Qur'an 2:34)*

Some of them said that the prostration was to Allah, and that Adam was only a *qiblah* (direction of prostration) for them. If this was correct, Allah would have said, 'Prostrate yourselves towards Adam', not ﴾'Prostrate yourselves before [lit. to] Adam.'﴿

If what had been meant was taking Adam as a *qiblah*, *Iblees* would not have refused to prostrate, and he would not have claimed that he was better than Adam, because the *qiblah* is only a direction, and taking it as a *qiblah* does not mean that it is regarded as superior.

It is true that the angels' prostration to Adam was an act of worship to Allah and obedience to Him, an action by which they drew closer to Him. But it was also an act of honour, respect and veneration towards Adam.

It is not reported that Adam prostrated to the angels. Adam and his descendents are not commanded to prostrate towards anyone except Allah, the Lord of the Worlds, because they – and Allah knows best – are the noblest of all creatures, i.e., the righteous son of Adam are the noblest of all creatures. There is no one above the righteous sons of Adam who prostrate none but Allah and prostrate with the best prostrations.

2 - Allah says that *Iblees* said:

﴿أَرَءَيْتَكَ هَٰذَا ٱلَّذِى كَرَّمْتَ عَلَىَّ ﴿٦٢﴾﴾

﴾'See this one whom You have honoured above me.'﴿

(Qur'an 17:62)

This clearly shows that Adam was honoured over *Iblees* when the latter was commanded to prostrate to him.

3 - Allah created Adam with His hand, whereas He created the angels by His word.

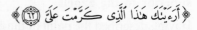

4 - Allah says:

﴿إِنِّي جَاعِلٌ فِي ٱلْأَرْضِ خَلِيفَةً ﴿٣٠﴾﴾

﴾I will create a vicegerent [*khaleefah*] on earth.﴿

(Qur'an 2:30 - A. Yoosuf 'Ali translation)

The one who is a *khaleefah* is superior to the one who is not a *khaleefah*. The angels asked that they might also become *khaleefahs* when they said,

﴿أَتَجْعَلُ فِيهَا مَن يُفْسِدُ فِيهَا وَيَسْفِكُ ٱلدِّمَآءَ ﴿٣٠﴾﴾

﴾Will You place therein those who will make mischief therein and shed blood...?﴿ *(Qur'an 2:30)*

If being a *khaleefah* had not been a high status, higher than their own, they would not have asked for it and felt envious of the one who had this status.

5 - The sons of Adam are superior to the angels in terms of knowledge. When Allah asked them (the angels) about the names of things, they could not answer and they acknowledged that they did not know them, and Adam told them the names. Allah says:

﴿هَلْ يَسْتَوِي ٱلَّذِينَ يَعْلَمُونَ وَٱلَّذِينَ لَا يَعْلَمُونَ ﴿٩﴾﴾

﴾Say: 'Are those who know equal to those who know not?'﴿

(Qur'an 39:9)

6 - Another indication of man's superiority is that man's obedience to Allah is more difficult, and that which is more difficult to fulfil is dearer when fulfilled. Man is inclined towards his physical desires, greed, anger and whims, and these things are not present in the angels.

7 - The *salaf* used to narrate *aḥaadeeth* which spoke of the superiority of righteous human beings over the angels. These reports were narrated openly to people. Had this been wrong they would have denounced it. This indicates that this was their belief.

8 - Allah praises them (righteous human beings) before His angels. Allah praises His slaves to the angels when they do anything that He has enjoined upon them or commanded them to do. When they perform an obligatory prayer, He praises them to the angels. In *Al-Musnad* and Ibn Maajah it is narrated from 'Abd-Allah that the Messenger (ﷺ) said: "Rejoice, for your Lord has opened one of the gates of heaven and is praising you to the angels. He is saying, 'Look at My slaves; they have done one duty and are waiting for the next.'"[5]

It is narrated from Abu Hurayrah that the Messenger (ﷺ) said: "Allah praises the people of *'Arafaat* to the people of heaven. He says to them: 'Look at My slaves. They have come to Me dusty and dishevelled (from travel).'" Its *isnaad* is *ṣaḥeeḥ* and it is narrated by Ibn Ḥibbaan in his *Ṣaḥeeḥ*, and by Al-Ḥaakim and by Al-Bayhaqi in *As-Sunan*.[6]

Those who regard the angels as superior quote for example the hadith, "Whoever remembers Me to himself, I will remember him to Myself, and whoever mentions Me in a gathering, I will mention him in a gathering better than it."

They also quote as evidence the fact that there are failings and shortcomings among the sons of Adam, and that they make errors and commit mistakes. And they quote *aayaat* such as,

﴿وَلَآ أَقُولُ لَكُمْ إِنِّى مَلَكٌ ﴿٥٠﴾﴾

﴾Nor I tell you that I am an angel.﴿ *(Qur'an 6:50)*

This indicates that the angels are better than humans.

The correct view

The matter may be resolved in the manner suggested by Ibn Taymiyah, who said that righteous human beings will be better in the end, when they enter Paradise, attain near access to Allah (38:25), dwell in the

5 *Ṣaḥeeḥ al-Jaami'*, 1/67.

6 *Ṣaḥeeḥ al-Jaami'*, 2/141.

highest levels, are greeted by the Most Merciful, are brought even closer, Allah manifests Himself to them and they have the joy of looking upon His Noble Face, and the angels will stand to serve them by the permission of their Lord.

But the angels are better at the beginning, for the angels now are closer to Allah. They are above the things that the sons of Adam indulge in, and they are devoted to the worship of their Lord. Undoubtedly at this point their situation is more perfect than that of mankind.

Ibn al-Qayyim said: With this explanation the issue of superiority becomes clear and the evidence of both parties is reconciled, and the view of each is shown to be acceptable to some extent.[7] And Allah knows best.

---

[7] For more information on this matter, see: *Majmoo' al-Fataawa*, 11/350; *Lawaami' al-Anwaar al-Bahiyyah*, 2/368; *Sharḥ al-'Aqeedah aṭ-Ṭaḥḥaawiyyah*, 338. Suyooṭi's book *Al-Ḥabaa'ik fi Akhbaar al-Malaa'ik* has also been published, in which there is a lengthy discussion (Pp. 203-251) of whether the angels or the sons of Adam are superior.

SYMBOLS' DIRECTORY

(سبحانه وتعالى) : *Subḥaanahu wa Ta'aala* - "The Exalted."

(صلى الله عليه وسلم) : *Ṣalla-Allahu 'Alayhi wa Sallam* -
"Blessings and Peace be upon him."

(عليه السلام) : *'Alayhis-Salaam* - "May Peace be upon him."

(رضي الله عنه) : *Raḍi-Allahu 'Anhu* - "May Allah be pleased with him."

(رضي الله عنها) : *Raḍi-Allahu 'Anha* - "May Allah be pleased with her."

GLOSSARY

Al-Ghayb	الغيب	:	The unseen
'Aqeedah	العقيدة	:	Faith, Creed
Al-Mulk	المُلك	:	Sovereignty
Al-Qadar	القدر	:	Divine decree, predestination
Al-Bayt al-Ma'moor	البيت المعمور	:	The much-frequented house; Ka'bah for the angels in the heaven above the Ka'bah in Makkah
'Ateed	عتيد	:	Ready
Assalamu 'Alaykum	السلام عليكم	:	Peace be upon you
'Alaqah	علقة	:	Clot
'Aṣr	عصر	:	Afternoon, time, Afternoon prayer
Al-Lawḥ al-Maḥfooẓ	اللوح المحفوظ	:	The Preserved Tablet
Al-Khandaq	الخندق	:	The Ditch
Ameen	آمين	:	Trustworthy
'Adn	عدن	:	A garden in Paradise
Al-Maseeḥ ad-Dajjaal	المسيح الدجال	:	The Pseudo-Christ; Pseudo Messiaḥ
Bayt al-'Izzah	بيت العِزة	:	The House of Glory
Bid'ah	بدعة	:	Reprehensible innovation in religion, heresy

Dhikr	الذِكر	:	Rememberance
Du'aa'	دعاء	:	Supplication
Eemaan	إيمان	:	Faith, belief
Fajr	الفجر	:	Dawn, dawn prayer
Faḥshaa'	فحشاء	:	Evil-deed, illegal sexual intercourse, sin, obscene
Ḥaraam	حرام	:	Prohibited
Ḥasanah	حسنة	:	Good deed
Iblees	ابليس	:	Satan
Iḥsaan	احسان	:	Perfection, Good
Ilaah	إله	:	God, diety
Israa'	إسراء	:	Night Journey
'Ishaa'	عِشاء	:	Night, Evening prayer
Insha' Allah	انشاء الله	:	God willing
Junub	جُنُب	:	In a state of ritual impurity following marital relations or sensuous dreams.
Khaleefah	خليفة	:	Vicegerent, Caliph, Deputy
Kiraaman	كِراما	:	Honourable
Kaatibeen	كاتبين	:	Scribes
Laḥd	لحد	:	Niche for the corpse
Maalik	مالِك	:	Owner, name of the incharge of Hell
Malak	مَلَك	:	Angel
Malaa'ik	ملائِك	:	Angels

Mi'raaj	معراج	: Ascent of the Prophet to the heavens
Mushrik	مشرك	: Polytheist
Muḍghah	مضغة	: Chewed lump of flesh
Maghrib	مغرب	: Sunset prayer, sunset
Miḥraab	محراب	: A praying place or a private room, niche
Mujrimoon	مجرمون	: Sing. *Mujrim*. Criminals, disbelievers, sinners
Nuṭfah	نطفة	: Embryo, mixed discharge from male and female
Qareen	قرين	: Constant Companion
Qa'eed	قَعيد	: Sitting
Qaṣab	قصب	: Pipes made of gold or pearls and other precious stones
Qiblah	قبله	: Direction of prostration during prayer, Ka'bah
Riḍwaan	رضوان	: Name of the angel in charge of Paradise
Raqeeb	رقيب	: Watcher
Ruqyah	رقية	: Amulet
Rooḥ al-Qudus	رُوح القدس	: Archangel Gabriel
Salaam	سلام	: Greetings
Sidrat al-Muntaha	سِدرة المنتهى	: The Lotus Tree of the utmost boundry over the seventh heaven beyond which no one can pass

Ṣaḥaabah	صحابة	:	Sing. *Ṣaḥaabi* The Prophet's Companions
Sakeenah	سكينة	:	Peace, tranquility
Ṣalaah	صلاة	:	Prayer, (obligatory/optional)
Ṣafara'	صفراء	:	Yellow
Tasbeeḥ	تسبيح	:	To say, *'Subḥaan Allah'*
Ṭawaaf	طواف	:	To go round (the Ka'bah), circumambulation
Thiqaat	ثقات	:	Sing. *Thiqah* Trustworthy
Taboot	تابوت	:	A wooden box, refers to the box that contained the relics of the Prophet Moses
Ṭaloot	طالوت	:	Qur'anic name for Saul
Ummah	أمه	:	Nation
Umm al-Mu'mineen	أم المؤمنين	:	The mother of the believers, (The Prophet's wife)
'Uboodiyyah	عبودية	:	Being a slave of Allah in the fullest sense
Wuḍoo'	وضوء	:	Ablution (ritual cleansing)
Waḥy	وحي	:	Revelation
Ẓaalimoon	ظالمون	:	Sing. *Ẓaalim*. Wrongdoers and polytheists, tyrants
Ẓuhr	ظهر	:	Noon, midday, midday prayer

TRANSLITERATION CHART

أ	a
آ . ى	aa
ب	b
ت	t
ة	h or t (when followed by another Arabic word)
ث	th
ج	j
ح	ḥ
خ	kh
د	d
ذ	dh
ر	r
ز	z
س	s
ش	sh
ص	ṣ
ض	ḍ
ط	ṭ

ظ	ẓ
ع	‘
غ	gh
ف	f
ق	q
ك	k
ل	l
م	m
ن	n
هـ – ه – ـه	h
و	w
و (as vowel)	oo
ي	y
ي (as vowel)	ee
ء	’ (Omitted in initial position)

ـَ	Fatḥah	a
ـِ	Kasra	i
ـُ	Ḍammah	u
ـّ	Shaddah	Double letter
ـْ	Sukoon	Absence of vowel